Tineke and Joep Bartels

# RIDE HORSES WITH AWARENESS AND FEEL

The New Dressage Training System from the Dutch Olympians at Academy Bartels

**With commentary by Imke Schellekens-Bartels**
*Silver Medalist 2008 Beijing Olympics*

Translated by Marji McFadden, M.A.

J.A. Allen • London

First published in 2008 by
J. A. Allen
45–47 Clerkenwell Green
London EC1R 0HT

J.A. Allen is an imprint of Robert Hale Ltd

www. halebooks.com

ISBN: 978-0-85131-963-6

Originally published in the Dutch language as *Bewuster Paardrijden* by Forte Uitgevers BV, Postbus 1273, 3890 BB Zeewolde, The Netherlands, 2006

Copyright © 2006 Forte Uitgevers BV, Zeewolde

English translation © 2008 Trafalgar Square Books

**Library of Congress Cataloguing in Publication Data**
A catalogue record for this book is available from the British Library.

Photo credits: Academy Bartels, Hooge Mierde (pp. 5, 26, 30, 32, 47, and 58); Arnd Bronkhorst, Garderen (pp. 6, 13, 35, 36, 50, 64, 65 right, 71 right, 76, 79, 80, 81, 83, 86, 87, 93, 96, 99, 105, 109, 110, 115, 118, 120, 124, and 132); KNHS (p. 56); and Dirk Caremans, Hemiksen (all other pages).

Illustration credits: Ed Boelaarts, De eurne

Book design by Het vlakke land, Rotterdam
Cover design by Heather Mansfield
Typefaces: Myriad Pro, Adobe Caslon Pro

**Printed in China**

# Contents

*The Academy Bartels team, from left to right: Joep, Imke, and Tineke.*

# Foreword

## The Academy's Tenth Year

We talk about horses almost all the time here at the Academy. My mother, Tineke, stands by the arena every morning to help and coach me. Tineke studied at the Academy for Physical Education and has a practical orientation. Furthermore, she is a very level-headed person. She is a former Olympic dressage rider and understands the experiences of rider and horse like no other.

My father, Joep, is a psychologist. He is interested in the mental processes of the rider and horse. He does not help me with training because we are too much alike. We are both fanatics, so I do better with a coach who is less intense and keeps me in check. However, my father is the person who always comes up with new ideas and keeps bringing different experts to the Academy.

My father is the researcher and author in the family. He writes about the things we discuss, which led to this second book from the Academy—the result of the collaboration between ourselves, the Academy team, and external experts, some of whom I think have also become part of our family. It is, in particular, the result of our practical experiences. We have extensively tested the training system we outline.

## Riding with Greater Awareness

Our Olympic experience, as well as teaching hundreds of "ordinary" riders at our training sessions, has convinced us that riding with greater awareness yields better results and makes riding more fun. In this book, we try to explain how you can learn to better understand a horse by being aware of its nature and origin; how you need to know and develop yourself by looking closely in the mirror; and how you should train with more awareness using four steps. These are: Action (Please do it), Pressure (Do it now!), Reaction (response), and Reward (Thank you). (See the Question and Answer Method on p. 82). We attempt to explain how you can refine communication with your horse and how, as a rider or trainer, you can make your horse a "happy athlete" (see p. 9) by challenging him "to seek reward." Contrast this concept with horses that "take flight from punishment."

Our views on training both horse and rider have advanced considerably in the past 10 years as a result of collaborating with experts in the

Netherlands and abroad, and through working knowledge of the sport. After watching my mother ride in four Olympic Games, my own dream became a reality when I successfully competed in the Athens and Beijing Olympics. However, our experience with "ordinary" enthusiastic riders, who take private lessons with us or participate in our training sessions, is just as valuable as our own competitive success. Their questions and comments at the end of a lesson and their enthusiasm are an important motivation for us to continue.

## New Discoveries

This new Academy book is an account of our discoveries over the past 10 years, and how these have led us to change our training system. Tineke completed her Master Coach training through the Dutch Olympic Committee institute. Our relationship and collaboration with freestyle groundwork trainer Emiel Voest was important because our training starts with the nature of the horse. Joep worked on mental coaching projects with Peter Murphy, former volleyball coach and NOC*NSF Sports Consulting staff, and sports psychologist Rico Schuijers. I learned the value of mental coaching in Athens, where I greatly benefited from the private training I received from Rico. Australian trainer Richard Weis, an expert on the independent seat and movement therapy, regularly came to the Academy. We also benefited from the excellent advice of Australian behavior expert and trainer Andrew McLean, as well as Dutch researcher Machteld van Dierendonck. As mentioned already, what is most useful for the average rider is the logical structure and clarity of the four steps of the teaching system: Action, Pressure, Reaction, and Reward.

However, there was another important impetus for developing the training system we use at the Academy. In recent years, my mother and I have trained regularly with Olympic champion Anky van Grunsven and have studied her approach as best we can. Anky's training method and those of other Olympic champions, such as Isabell Werth and Nicole Uphoff, were the subject of endless discussions with top trainers from around the world who stayed at the Academy to participate in the Global Dressage Forum. These were often heated and lasted late into the night. We now use a lot of what we have learned from Anky, even when we teach beginner riders. We have not broken away from the classical system of training—in which my mother was trained, too—but we have modified that system, and we have advanced. We find it interesting that the main subject of attention when the discussion of "riding deep and round" comes up in the horse world is the horse's head position, while the goal of the Academy Bartels training method—improving the horse's gymnastic development and eliminating mental and physical blockages—is talked about far less.

## Riding with "Feel"

We thought it was time to write a book on developments in international training systems. Many misunderstandings have arisen about training horses. Perhaps not every rider can implicitly copy the practical methods of successful riders such as Nicole Uphoff, Isabell Werth, Ulla Salzgeber, and Anky van Grunsven; however, we can learn a great deal from their methods. I believe the fact that all these riders are female is related to their success. Equestrian sport stems from military tradition. In the past, riders were mainly strong men. Women have less physical strength but generally ride with more "feel," which has made dressage more beautiful. Nevertheless, there are critics who still believe that the riding techniques of men—as seen in classical riding—are better than the methods shown by "sensitive" women. We disagree. We feel that riding is better today than it was in the past and both the quality of horses and training methods have improved. The lower levels are also better than they used to be. We know this well because hundreds of riders take our courses each year.

We believe it is important to explain the basic principles of our training system, describing not just the advantages but also the pitfalls and dangers. Riding deep is just one small detail of a complete system and is no guarantee of success in itself, as bad or good riding bears no direct relationship to a horse's neck position. You can ride classically very well and ride deep very poorly; however, riding deep very well has produced the best results for many years.

We are convinced that innovation in training horses for sport is still in its infancy. Riders in the Netherlands pay a great deal of attention to new developments and we at the Academy are involved too. We greatly enjoyed writing this book because we like informing other riders of these new ideas in training. Perhaps we will have something like a "Dutch dressage school" in the future, in which case we will no longer need to use the German word *Durchlässigkeit* to describe the goal of our training; instead, we can just say that we want our horse to be "open" to the rider. Our theme in all that we do is to learn more and keep developing; it is the Academy's trademark. If we continue to develop, we will, we hope, stay of interest to our students and guests. However, our pursuits have an additional benefit as I am truly convinced that riding with greater awareness is also more effective, comfortable, and fun for both you and your horse!

*Imke Schellekens-Bartels*
Silver medal winner 2008 Beijing Olympics

*Imke with Lancet at the Athens Olympics (sire: Wenzel x Shogun xx, owners: Stal Bartels and Coomans, Maree and Brinkman). When riding goes this well, it is as if you are on automatic pilot. Your "conscious" training and preparation leads to an "unconscious" performance. You do not have to think about riding anymore.*

## CHAPTER I

# From Conscious to Subconscious Riding

## From Communication to Rider "Feel"

Riding is an action sport, one that is about the body and "feel." For the most part, riding is done subconsciously; you do it with your body, reflexes, feel, and subconscious ("automatic pilot," as we call it in this book). Riders with world-class talent "just do it" and make riding look like it happens automatically. Tineke and Imke do not consider themselves world-class talent, and they work with hundreds of people each year who take courses at the Academy, most of whom do not have this sort of talent. In all these cases, riding is not a matter of just doing it—riding must be learned. At least, that is what Tineke and Imke have experienced, and this is what you may find out, too.

Learning takes place consciously, but oddly enough, we have to learn many things consciously that we later have to perform subconsciously, things that we no longer have to think about. Riding with more awareness should ultimately lead to "subconscious" riding—riding on automatic pilot, which is something you attain step by step by learning more about your horse and yourself. The so-called "classical literature" on riding pays relatively little attention to what we consider important matters such as "conscious" and "unconscious" behavior; the nature of the horse; communication with a "flight animal"; rider psychology; and rider feel. Fortunately, modern equestrian thought has led to more attention being paid to these areas. Riding is not a purely technical endeavor and riding skill does not exist without feel. A feel for riding can be instilled by following the steps below, which are outlined in this book by chapter in the same order:

- Learning to communicate with a flight animal and herd animal
- Developing self-knowledge and self-control
- Developing body control, body language, and an independent seat
- Learning to give effective aids by training with the Question and Answer method
- Developing rider feel

*Emiel Voest with Tineke's new mare Toscane (sire: Krack C x Oracle, owners: Stal Bartels and J. van Eekeren). In recent years, this "freestyle" trainer has been involved in training and giving courses at the Academy. In this book, we give a great deal of consideration to his views on communication between people and horses.*

## Communicating with a Flight Animal

The number of people who come to us who want to learn how to ride continues to grow; however, many people do not really know what kind of animal a horse is. Everything you do has to start with the horse. A horse is not a human and should not be treated like one. A horse is a "prey animal," which is also "flight animal"; in contrast, people are "predatory animals." Fortunately, both horses and people are "herd animals," so we actually have something in common. Hierarchy is very important to herd animals, and absolute obedience to higher ranking animals helps increase chances for survival. Obedience does not have to be forced; horses freely accept it. Young animals are also raised this way, learning how to act out of respect for the experience and knowledge of a higher ranking animal.

People can learn to use their sense of hierarchy inherent in herd animals, as we rank above horses. It is unproductive, even dangerous, when a horse does not accept you as his leader—a principle that should always be kept in mind. By definition, communication problems exist between animals of different species. In fact, there is no greater difference than the one between predatory animals and prey animals where there are completely opposing interests. Therefore, it comes as no surprise that communication differs among species and that these differences can lead to confusion.

Even so, communication between people and horses is certainly possible because horses are true team players. This interaction for the most part is dependent on body language. We have the advantage of learning how to adapt our body language to that of horses. Although we can never completely match theirs, we can certainly approach it. To best use our body, we must rely on our ability to observe our horse's reactions and translate them correctly. In short, we must ask ourselves what we are saying with our body language, and what the horse means when he reacts to it with a certain behavior.

## Develop Self-Knowledge

A horse always sees through you and gives you what you are. To ride well, you first have to know yourself. Most people do not know themselves well at all. Our students are sometimes surprised when, after taking the psychological tests at the Academy, they are faced with aspects of their personalities of which they were previously unaware. We always advise people to be honest and regularly "look in the mirror." You have to know your weak points in order to work on them. You also have to learn to use your body consciously—whether working your horse in hand or under saddle.

We often see a situation dealt with by a rider from an unconscious-incompetence position. To explain: we make a mistake (incompetence), but we do not realize we did something wrong (unconscious). The main result of this is mutual misunderstanding, which can subsequently lead to a complete breakdown in communication. This concept applies both under saddle and in hand. Sometimes, a rider gets frustrated, which is understandable. In fact, even Grand Prix riders get frustrated! It is a big transition to go from riding a top Olympic horse to riding a young horse that bucks or does not want to work. Most riders experience feelings of disappointment and frustration at some point.

Almost all of us have tried to force something by using strength and haste, which is deadly in equestrian sports. Nothing can be forced; everything must be based on patience. The "longest" way is, ultimately, the shortest. So, banish all force and tension, and be positive. Training is only effective when you approach it with a positive attitude. Tell the horse what he *should* do; do not tell him what he *should not* do. Force is not part of the equation. You need patience, self-discipline, and a great deal of technical knowledge and expertise to train horses. Furthermore, you must continue to strive to improve yourself as a rider and trainer.

Riding affects you at a very deep level, and touches the essence of your being. It also makes you humble: just when you feel that you have finally "arrived," it has a way of sending you back to "square one." For this

The horse is a herd animal, a true team player, and is sensitive to ranking hierarchy. As leader of the human-equine team, you rank above your horse. Leadership depends on body language. People have the advantage of learning how to adapt their body language to that of the horse. However, you first have to understand the horse's body language.

reason, it is useful to approach riding with humility. For more than 30 years, Tineke has ridden seven or eight horses a day, worked seven days a week, and listened to the best trainers in the world, and we at the Academy still do not think we know it all. Our motto is "keep learning." We take this attitude because we frequently find that we are dependent on the horse we are riding at the moment. When a horse is sold or retired, it means starting all over again. Although these transitions can be humbling, they encourage us to persist and persevere. We consider the enjoyment of learning more important than the pursuit of success. We always view improving both a young horse and ourselves as a challenge, and we think this attitude should be adhered to by every rider and trainer. Having a career in riding means you must prepare for lifelong learning—not only physically but also psychologically. However, mental growth can only take place when you have a foundation of self-knowledge. For these reasons, "looking in the mirror" regularly and listening to what others have to say are very important.

## Body Control: Learning How to Sit

Communication from the saddle works according to the same principles as communication from the ground but is dependent on totally different signals. You are barely visible to the horse when in the saddle, but he can feel and hear you. Your voice is perhaps the only ground aid that you take with you when you get on the horse. After that, good riding depends on body and voice control. You can only give the correct aids when you can consciously control and coordinate your body and voice. It is vital that you have this body control before you can begin training the horse and developing your rider "feel."

Body control does not depend on a specific position but on balance instead. Riding is a balancing act, which you can only attain when you know and can control your body. A supple and unforced rider's seat is the foundation on which every horse's every performance is based. Your seat should primarily depend on dynamic balance, not on a "textbook" position that, though appearing "correct," is actually stiff. It is possible to have a textbook-perfect seat yet not be able to influence your horse. In our last book, we called this kind of rider "an old stick," that is, someone who is correct "by the book," but without necessary feel.

An independent seat, however, is one of the most important basic principles on which you develop rider feel and learn to ride well. Your core (the Germans use the word *Mittelpositur*) consists of your seat, pelvis, and stomach. Your seat "sticks" to the saddle, while your upper body, hands, and lower legs, though kept as still as possible, remain relaxed and independent from the core. Developing a stable core is mainly accomplished by learning to follow the horse's movement, which is best learned by sitting as quietly as you can. It may be surprising that a rider

*The Australian instructor Richard Weis believes that your body is the instrument with which you can get the horse to do what you want. To use it well, you must have an independent seat: you must first train yourself in order to train your horse!*

with a correct seat looks more like he is standing with his legs slightly apart and bent, not like he is sitting! You must realize that your body is the instrument you use to ask your horse to do what you want: for example, you have the means to ask him to not only perform specific exercises but also to be more supple or produce more impulsion—all this just from using your body's good "spring action."

## Training with the Question and Answer Method

If you want to achieve something with your horse, you have to know how he best learns. Much has already been written about the end result: a horse that performs well and/or a rider with a good seat. However, far less is known about the learning process and exactly how you should teach your horse the skills you want him to have. In this book, we give a great deal of attention to the horse's learning process.

A horse can learn from several training methods including Habituation, Operant Conditioning, and Classical Conditioning. The second method, Operant Conditioning, which we utilize, is also known as training by trial and error; however, we prefer to call it training with the Question and Answer method. In practice, first, you ask a horse to do something by giving him a signal. When the horse does not understand or respond to this aid, then you challenge him by putting pressure on in the form of another request, and removing this pressure the moment he reacts. The process pretty much works as follows: when you want your horse to go forward from a leg aid, first touch him with both legs. If that has no effect, challenge him with more encouragement by using a stronger leg aid or even your spur or your whip. He will then try to get rid of that pressure by reacting. (Note: in this book, we sometimes use the words "encourage" and "challenge" when dealing with the concept of "pressure.")

You challenge your horse to find the key with which he can remove that pressure. The moment your horse reacts, immediately remove the pressure by letting your legs hang relaxed on the horse's sides and relaxing your hands. This is the reward. You can also reward your horse with your voice, a pat on the neck, or a stroke on his crest. The removal of pressure when he reacts in the right way will be remembered after a few repetitions. This method teaches a horse in a positive way: he does not go forward as a reaction to the rider's leg or spurs; he does so because he knows that he will be rewarded as a result. It is easy to test the effectiveness of your aids: you know they are working when you get an increasingly quick reaction from your horse from using increasingly less pressure.

The four steps of the Question and Answer method are: Action, Pressure, Reaction, and Reward. Over time, you will merely need to give an aid—the Action step; application of Pressure will not be necessary. You will just ask and your horse will answer with his Reaction.

*Andrew and Manuele McLean (on the right) during a visit to Academy Bartels. These Australian trainers and behavioral scientists acquainted us with "learning" theory. They introduced us to the concepts—Action, Pressure, Reaction, and Reward—on which the Academy's teaching method is based.*

The four steps of the game of Question and Answer are: Action, Pressure, Reaction, and Reward. Training with this method goes like this: you give your horse an aid (the Action step) of leg pressure to move forward. If your horse does not react, then you challenge him (the Pressure step) by repeating the same aid but stronger. The moment your horse answers correctly (the Reaction), immediately cease your aid and relax your hand. This is the Reward step, and the horse will remember the praise after a few repetitions, with the result that in the future the horse will go forward when you ask because he knows that he will be rewarded when he does.

## Riding with "Feel"

Anyone who has ever experienced riding a horse that is totally "through" and using his back optimally never forgets it. It is a feeling that you always want to return. The memory of this perfect "rider feel" is your training goal; however, expressing this concept in words is not easy, which in turn, makes it difficult to explain to students. You have to experience it.

Riding with feel is largely an unconscious act. It allows you to communicate with your horse without having to think. Rider feel facilitates increasingly refined communication where you allow your horse to open himself to the aids in complete trust. The German Training Scale uses the word *Durchlässigkeit* (letting through) to describe a horse in this state. We prefer to say the horse is "open." The horse opens his whole body and mind to the rider. It is a state of mind; the horse feels safe with his rider. Openess is also a matter of psychological and physical maturity. It occurs when all blockages in a horse's body and mind are gone. Eliminating these blockages is the rider's job.

What is a blockage or block? According to Tineke, a blockage occurs when a horse braces some part of his body. Blockages can have a mental or a physical cause. Some horses lose their confidence in a certain position, situation, or exercise. They get stiff and tighten their body. Physical reasons for blockages stem from discomfort or pain. If a horse is experiencing pain, he reacts to it by tensing his muscles.

RIDE HORSES WITH AWARENESS AND FEEL

A horse is many times stronger than a rider, so attempting to get rid of muscle tension through force is futile. The best way to eliminate a block is to deal with it like a mental coach, fitness trainer, or physical therapist and come up with appropriate mental and gymnastic exercises for your horse's problem. Then apply the exercises with great patience and increase their difficulty step by step. This training process will gradually make your horse "looser" and stronger—and you will win his trust.

When you have reached the stage where your horse is open to you, teaching him movements or asking for collection ceases to be an issue—it just happens naturally. We know this sounds like a fairy tale. Many young riders have a hard time believing top riders when they say that they spend the majority of their time working on the basics and the rest happens on its own. But it is the truth! A horse that is open naturally collects himself. A horse is only comfortable to ride when he has nothing blocking him. To achieve this, we at the Academy train many horses with our system that encourages the horse to go in a deep and round neck position. (For more, see p. 119).

We do not use this system with all horses and all riders. Furthermore, the way in which you train deep and round is very important: our goal is to have the horse "let his head fall," so to speak, of his own free will. Pulling the neck "round" is wrong; the horse must become accustomed slowly and subsequently give the rider the feeling that he enjoys it and is feeling "safe" in this position. When training, the deeper head position can be alternated with a higher one, and a shorter neck position alternated with a longer one; as a result, training also functions as a gymnastic exercise.

Scientific research has shown the positive effects of training deep and round, *provided it is done correctly*. Riders and trainers who use this method responsibly have learned from experience that it makes their horses relaxed, loose, and obedient. In the Netherlands, the method is continually evolving. Perhaps in the future we will talk about the "Dutch school of dressage."

Of course, good results can be achieved with other training systems, when applied correctly, as has been proven in the past. However, it is remarkable that all the major competitions in the past decades have been won by riders who train their horses deep and round. In our approximately 40-year career in competitive dressage, we at the Academy believe that training deep and round has real benefits.

Most of our horses and those of our students develop for the better. They become looser, suppler, lighter in the hand, physically stronger, and nicer to ride. As your horse's fitness trainer and physical therapist, you can "massage away," as it were, all blockages. Horses "move over the back" better, in particular. They can elevate their forehands more easily and be more supple through their body better when they are in the classical position for show. In addition, they become more beautiful, better muscled, and friendlier on the ground. In the saddle, you will notice that your horse accepts you as his leader and totally trusts you. He enjoys following your directions and feels confident and safe. Perhaps this is so because "force" in the form of spurs or the whip (the Pressure) is needed less often—the horse reacts correctly to the first aid. The rider-horse hierarchy is being established in a playful way.

The objectives of the Academy Bartels training method fit completely with the rules of the international equestrian sports organization, the FEI (Fédération Equestre Internationale). The ideal image of the horse is clearly stated in these rules. Training must develop a dressage horse into a "happy athlete through harmonious education."

The aim of our training method is clearly stated in the international dressage rulebook, which describes the ideal dressage horse as a "happy athlete." A happy athlete "opens" himself both physically and mentally to you, making you believe that he feels totally safe with you. As your horse's fitness trainer and physical therapist, you can "massage away," so to speak, all blockages—physical or mental. The horse's expression, muscling, and movement will show you that he has become a happy, harmoniously developed athlete.

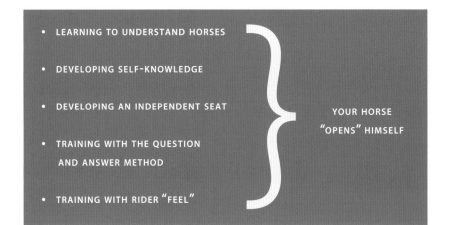

- LEARNING TO UNDERSTAND HORSES
- DEVELOPING SELF-KNOWLEDGE
- DEVELOPING AN INDEPENDENT SEAT
- TRAINING WITH THE QUESTION AND ANSWER METHOD
- TRAINING WITH RIDER "FEEL"

} YOUR HORSE "OPENS" HIMSELF

Emiel Voest has shown us the
differences and the similarities
between people and horses. A horse
is a "prey animal" and therefore
a "flight animal"; a person is a
"predatory animal." Fortunately, we
are both "herd animals." This is the
starting point of the training method
developed at the Academy. As herd
animals, horses are true team players.
To make the most of this quality,
people need to adapt to horses.

## CHAPTER 2
# Learning to Understand Horses

### Horses Are Not People

Actually, good riding is nothing more than a big journey while discovering the nature of the horse. We will attempt to explain how this journey has unfolded over the past years by presenting a number of examples. Emiel Voest has played an important part in this. Emiel calls himself "a freestyle groundwork trainer without the hocus-pocus." He prefers not to use the term "horse whisperer" because his way of dealing with horses is not mysterious—something that this term indeed suggests. Emiel combines others' ideas and customizes them for his students.

"There are people who say, 'I want to deal with my horse on equal footing, but I want him to do what I say.' This is not possible. If you determine what the horse should do, then you cannot have an equal relationship. I believe that as soon as you start thinking about training a horse, leadership is the first step involved." Emiel believes the "new" thinking championed by the founders of these methods is actually not new at all: "It is the old way of dealing with horses in a new package. Horses often do better with those who practice 'traditional horsemanship'—people who do not tolerate a badly behaved horse and put a horse to work right away—than with people who play around with their horses as if they are stuffed animals. When people treat their horses like stuffed animals, they do not accept them for what they are, and furthermore, they give them unclear signals that horses cannot understand."

Our study of the horse's nature was fine-tuned by researcher Machteld van Dierendonck, whose work includes a multiple-year study of equine herd behavior, rank order, and leadership.

### The Horse Is More Natural than We Think

People regularly say that horses no longer respond in a natural way because they have functioned as work animals for generations. The following points help illustrate that horses are perhaps still more natural than we think:

- Horses have been in existence for approximately 70 million years. In this time, the original horse has evolved into a social grazing animal.

- *Genus equus* has been in existence for approximately 3 million years and is subdivided into three types of wild donkeys, three types of zebras, and the horse.
- Approximately one-and-a-half million years ago, the Przewalski horse and the domesticated horse became two distinct animals.
- People have used the domesticated horse over many thousands of years.

*We need to teach a horse how to relax anytime we want. This begins by teaching him to lower his head on command. A horse associates a low head position with relaxation and safety.*

Humans have influenced the horse's evolution for a relatively short time. It is clear that the horse's natural qualities are still very much present. According to equine experts, a horse's behavior is based on the following three facts, which are listed in order of importance as they relate to the horse's training: 1) prey animal; 2) herd animal; 3) flight animal. What does this actually mean for training horses? Prey animals are innately wary, which, when dealing with people, can be translated into suspicion. Emiel believes this behavior is entirely justified considering that people have been horses' greatest enemies for the last 100,000 years or so. People belong to the group of major predatory animals, which is why it is logical that horses initially have difficulty allowing us on their back. In the wild, an animal on his back is often the last thing a horse experiences before he is killed. It is indeed problematic that we want horses in this position to relax and give to the bit.

The implication for training is that we must learn not to behave like predators when we work with horses. Our body language and our way of moving are two of several important ways we can demonstrate we are not. A horse will sense any tension we have, and its response can easily be

*We also teach a horse to lower his head upon request under saddle, as shown here by Imke on Sunrise. She is doing this with a wide-and-low hand position that we will describe later in the book. Furthermore, she is doing this without force and pressure and in the normal course of training.*

People belong to the group of major predatory animals, which is why it is understandable that horses initially have difficulty allowing us on their back. In the wild, a predator on his back is often the last thing a horse experiences before he is killed. It is indeed problematic that we ask horses in this position to relax and give to the bit.

predicted. Therefore, relaxation must begin with the trainer or rider—not the horse. A horse can sense both tension and relaxation through our body language and movement.

## Spooking Is a Matter of Life and Death

As predatory animals, we often do not understand the reactions of prey animals very well because we view the world from a different perspective. When a predator hears something rustling in the trees, he thinks that that noise may be caused by something to eat. On the other hand, the prey animal shies from such a noise—jumping away or taking flight because hidden dangers can lurk in the woods. Matters of life and death for a horse are not always convenient for a rider: a horse that spooks constantly is not much fun to ride. Nevertheless, we see this behavior in some top dressage horses: Rembrandt, Bonfire, and Salinero are three such examples of recent Olympic champions. Our horse Barbria was also quite spooky.

Considering their wary nature, which compels them to watch for trouble and danger, it is logical that horses, in general, are almost always alert. They are also alert to other things, such as signals from other horses in the herd. Horses cannot allow themselves long, carefree periods of rest at night; moreover, they have to be extra watchful during twilight and at night. Horses sleep at most three hours out of a 24-hour day, divided over several periods, with a maximum of 20 minutes true REM sleep in each period. In addition, horses take periods during which they rest watchfully. On average, a mature horse in the wild rests or sleeps only about 20 percent of the time.

A horse also distinguishes between sleep and watchful rest when he is lying down. In general, we can say that a horse lying down with his head raised is resting watchfully, while a fully prostrate horse is often truly sleeping. A horse spends the remainder of his day moving, for which all his bodily functions are designed. Horses were not meant to spend 23 hours a day standing in a stall; allowing them as much movement as possible is best for their health. Consequently, horses that move about freely the entire day have the ability to go from a stand still to top speed within a few seconds when they are threatened with danger.

## Learn to Recognize the Flight Position

Flight is often preceded by the "flight position." This is the physical pose where a horse tenses his body, raises his neck, opens his eyes and nostrils wide, and pricks his ears straight forward. This position generates adrenaline production, among other chemicals, which a horse needs in times of flight. It is important that we learn to recognize all the signs of the flight position (also see Survival Techniques on p. 20). The sooner we see or feel that a horse is moving into the flight position, the easier it is to intervene.

The flight position is not limited to those signs just described; it can also be recognized by other physical signs, including tail swishing and head shaking. A horse may also "lock" his back and neck, snort, "lock" his mouth, open his eyes wide, prick his ears forward or pin them flat, and clamp his tail between his legs. Allow a horse in such a state to relax by keeping his head low or taking a break, and do not ask anything extra at such a time. If you do not recognize the flight position, the moment will come when the horse takes off just to burn off adrenaline. This usually comes as a total surprise! Therefore, it is very important that we learn the body language of horses, in general; and to learn the body language of our own horse extremely well, in particular.

## Rank Order and Leadership

The horse is ruled by fear. Fear of predators—in other words, fear of death—is serious fear! In the wild, a fearful horse often lives a long life. In short, our relationship with horses means always having to deal with the fear factor, which is the result of a basic survival mechanism. A horse that ranks high in his herd may be afraid to be a lead horse or to leave its territory alone. For people, this behavior seems contradictory, but it is not abnormal for horses. High ranking horses are those that win in horse against horse conflicts, which, incidentally, are usually settled with

*In principle, alert horses in tune with their surroundings can also learn to listen to their rider well. The rider needs to teach his horse to focus attention on him during training. In this photo, Sunrise's attention is still not entirely focused on Emiel Voest; she is much more interested in what is going on around her.*

little violence. It does not take long before one horse clearly shows he considers the other the higher ranking animal.

Rank order is somewhat different than leadership. Rank order happens between two animals. All horses follow the leader, but the leader is not necessarily the highest ranking horse. Leaders are often high ranking horses, but they have other qualities, too. They are the animals that literally and figuratively give direction to the daily rhythm of life. Leaders in the horse world generally occupy social functions. They are a bit older, have offspring (and therefore vested interests) in the herd, and as a result, have to be extra careful. Wariness or even fear in this context is very natural behavior. Horses are especially afraid of things they do not know; therefore, we need to be clear in our training and try to avoid causing fear. In chapter 5 on training, we discuss how we can best accomplish these tasks.

A horse that is constantly uneasy in his environment can be a challenge for a show rider, but this can also work to one's advantage because an attentive horse is also a lively and active animal. The FEI's implementation of the phrase "happy athlete" in its new rules as being the ideal in competitive dressage, once again underscores the thinking that it is better to have a lively and attentive horse than a "dead head." So we view wariness as a positive quality in a show horse: when such a horse is distracted by his surroundings, it is the job of the trainer to harness the horse's ability to pay attention to details to his own advantage and focus the horse's attention on him and the work at hand. Whatever you do, be sure that your training methods never dull a horse's spirit. Avoid boring work!

Leadership and rank order play an important role in training; after all, a horse pays attention to the lead animal of the herd and the higher ranking animal nearby. As just mentioned, horses that pay close attention and are wary about their environment can, in theory, also learn to listen to the rider well. These are sensitive animals, usually. However, not everyone can train such a horse. Therefore, a less uneasy type—a quieter animal—is a better alternative for many riders.

## In a Panoramic Cinema

To explain a horse's reactions, we have to go back to his natural qualities and his sensory characteristics, one of which is eyesight. Horses possess unusual vision capabilities, which allow them to stay on constant alert and spot danger while they graze. Their eyes are placed on either side of their head, giving them an almost 360-degree view, except for a small area directly in front of their head and an area immediately behind them. However, with a small movement of the head, they can see in these areas, too.

It is difficult for us to understand how a horse sees. Imagine not having to turn our head to see what is behind us. What does a horse see when

We view wariness as a positive quality in a show horse. When a horse is distracted by external factors, it is the trainer's job to focus the horse's attention on him. The rider must take the horse's ability to focus on his surroundings and transfer this focus to the work at hand. Care must be taken when training such a sensitive horse to not destroy his spirit with dull, boring work.

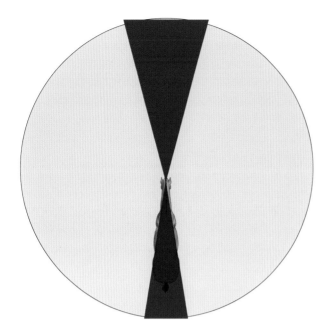

*With the exception of two small areas—one directly in front and one behind them, horses have an almost 360-degree field of vision, allowing them to be on constant alert and spot danger in a timely manner. Equine vision can perhaps best be compared to being a panoramic cinema.*

something is happening on his left side at the same time that something different is happening on his right? Does a horse see the same things left and right, and what does the total picture look like? Emiel Voest says that a "panoramic view" may best describe the horse's vision. This clearly has far-reaching consequences for training. The horse has the perfect type of vision for a grazing animal; however, this ability to see in the context of the rider's environment exposes a horse to too much information, which is often incomprehensible, as well.

## Horses "Think" in Images

Horses probably think more in images than people do. If an image is not "right," then a horse becomes suspicious and afraid. A person who puts on a hat or cap is not always recognized as such but seen as a "new image." This is why horses often spook at things that people find difficult to understand unless they learn to think in images themselves. Horses see in the dark better than we do, although they adjust much more slowly to changes from dark to light and vice versa than people. Horses also have much less depth perception, which also makes sense, given that they are grazers and not hunters!

Besides the obvious consequences for training, it is important to realize that a horse has to learn everything from two sides. For example, a horse may completely accept a saddle being placed on his back from the left side and then spook at that same saddle when it is placed on his back from the right side. In tests, horses recognized objects with their right eye, which they had observed with their left eye. However, when a saddle is placed on a horse's back from the off-side, it is embedded in a different background, which the horse registers as a different total picture. Perhaps that is the crux of the matter. Horses probably see things this way because they lack lateral depth perception, which is why an indoor arena looks different to a horse tracking to the left than it does tracking right!

## Horses Are Team Players

There is strength in numbers. Knowing this, horses feel safer in the herd. It is important to realize that we can never give horses that feeling because we are a different species. What's more, we are essentially the very things they fear. However, we can certainly leverage the sense of hierarchy, connection, and cooperation inherent to herd animals. A well-functioning herd has "agreements," which also have to do with rank within the herd. Everyone has to know which horse is in charge in times of emergency—a decision greatly influenced by hierarchy. Absolute obedience to the signals of the higher ranking animals helps to increase chances for survival.

*Imke and Emiel have worked together several times on the ground. Groundwork provides practical insight into the fact that horses are good "team players." They are very happy to cooperate, provided there is mutual understanding. This understanding can be reached through the Question and Answer method—a "game" played with your body language and your horse (p. 77).*

Obedience is not coerced but accepted out of free will. Horses are true team players, and young animals are raised to become team players. They learn to act out of respect for the experience and knowledge of a higher ranking animal or leader. It is remarkable that determination of rank order is not coupled with a great deal of violence. Truly dominant animals usually do not need to use violence. A lowered neck or pinned ears is often more than enough to make clear the higher ranking animal's position.

Researcher Machteld van Dierendonck has observed that the best predictor of rank order is the lower ranking animal's willingness to move out of the space of another animal; as explained on p. 15, rank order is somewhat different than leadership. And not all horses in a herd share the same hierarchical relationship with say, the lead mare, as this mare is not equally dominant over every horse.

Furthermore, leadership depends on the particular situation. In cases of danger, a stallion may dominate over all horses in the herd but may not be boss when it comes to eating and drinking, which makes it difficult to see which horse is really the herd leader. A herd may actually include several leaders, which in scientific terms are referred to as "key animals."

Leadership in a herd is different from rank order. A leader is not necessarily the highest ranking horse. However, both terms point to a very important principle: horses are team players, and they feel safe with their group. Although people are different from horses, we can leverage the horse's inherent sense of hierarchy, connection, and cooperation. As team leader, you can make your horse feel safe.

## Communication Problems

Communication problems always exist between different species. For example, cats deal with one another differently than dogs, and this difference is clearest when you see a cat playing with a dog. The games that a dog thinks are fun a cat does not like at all, and vice versa. Cats and dogs have different ways of expressing their feelings: a dog with a rigid tail raised straight up is communicating "I'm very dominant;" while a cat with the same tail position is expressing something along the lines of "I like you a lot!"

Even greater than the difference between dogs and cats is the one between predatory animals and prey animals. The two have totally opposing interests, so it comes as no surprise that each species has a different way of communicating. For example, it is commonly known that you have a better chance of catching a horse by walking away from him than toward him: we instinctively want to approach the horse, a desire that is inherent in our predatory nature; however, if instead you walk away, he will probably follow you. In the end, you will get what you want: you will catch the horse and take him with you. Therefore, you must learn how to suppress your predatory reactions and adjust to the prey animal.

## What Is Learned Young Is Learned Well

Horses are precocious animals (*nidifugous*, which literally means "leaving the nest soon after hatching"). In other words, they are able to care for themselves to a certain extent immediately after they are born. This ability to exhibit mature qualities early is quite different from cats or dogs, which are born helpless and blind (not to mention a newborn baby). A herd animal of flight must possess several qualities soon after birth in order to survive—the first 24 hours of life are critical. We call this the imprint phase; a foal in this period of time must absorb a great deal of information without having it repeated many times. The foal's "hard drive" is open and data can be directly written onto it.

Foals learn in several ways: by copying the behavior of their dam and other members of the herd, and by falling and getting up through trial-and-error. Of course, horses are quickly able to learn these behaviors essential to their basic survival: eating, drinking, spooking, fleeing, and recognizing their dam and other horses. Their instinct drives them to find their dam's udder and they search everywhere until they finally find a teat. Once they accomplish this, they always know where to look.

Foals in this imprint phrase require far less repetition than do people to learn new things. We can use the imprint phase in training to give a foal

*A horse naturally pulls away against pressure, that is, when you tug on the lead rope, he will unconsciously throw up his head. This is an automatic reaction and is called an opposition reflex.*

several important experiences, such as getting used to physical contact with people, adjusting to noise, having its legs picked up, and, in particular, yielding to pressure (a response that is important for later training).

## Survival Techniques

To learn to understand a prey animal, you need to know the survival techniques you may have to deal with in the course of training. "The

Four Fs" stand for the order of the phases in which horses react when they are frightened:

1 Flight
2 Fight
3 Freeze
4 Faint

### 1  Flight

Flight is always a horse's first choice. When a horse spooks and runs off, he has chosen flight. If flight is not possible, a horse will have no other choice other than to fight or freeze. When he freezes, he becomes rigid with fear; the worst form of this is actually fainting. It is important in training that these signs are recognized early.

Examples of "flight behavior" in training include the horse moving out from under you in a walk-trot transition, dropping his back shortly before the transition, or raising his neck. Things usually start going wrong in the preparation for the transition. The moment just before the first flight signal is the point at which you have to make the correction—certainly not after the horse takes off! The best way to stop a horse from fighting or resisting is by sending him forward. If you allow the flight response and learn how to control it, you can prevent Phase 2 and 3. We make a distinction between guided flight (under the rider's control) and blind flight (bolting).

### 2  Fight

A horse will fight, for example, when he cannot escape what he feels is too much pressure from the bit, and therefore will start to shake or raise his head against the pressure from the hands. A horse fighting in this context initially uses his strength unconsciously. Resistance often works to a horse's advantage because he is stronger than we are. Once a horse learns he can benefit by resisting, he will then consciously use resistance to get his way. This situation tempts riders into using more force, which leads to a vicious circle that ultimately ends in anger and frustration. The horse will win this fight.

### 3  Freeze

Freezing is perhaps best translated as "resistance." If a horse does not get results by fleeing or fighting, he is faced with a dilemma. He does not know what to do at that point, so he blocks himself both emotionally and physically. Resistance is not obstinacy but powerlessness. It sometimes appears as "restricted awareness," when a horse can barely perceive stimulus from the environment, let alone process it. The rider's aids do not work, and the horse misinterprets them.

This restricted awareness is coupled with a physical sensory blockage. At this point, horses likely feel less physical sensation than normal, and commonly show little or no reaction to a smack of the whip (for example, when being loaded into a trailer). When this happens, it is also important to discover what the horse does before he resists, as that is the only point at which we can intervene. Be aware that fear plays a big role in resistance.

### 4 Faint

Horses do not faint like people do, although horses can "lose their minds" in extremely stressful situations. Freezing precedes fainting, the signs of which can also be recognized. One sign of fainting is loss of leg control (such as tripping or the legs completely folding). Practical examples include a horse that lies down because he is afraid of the trailer or one that suddenly lies down when he is put in harness.

Fainting is the final reaction of a frightened horse when nothing else has helped him. A horse in this phase is highly vulnerable and will only reach this point under extreme circumstances. Punishing a horse at this time is the worst possible action you can take, as the horse will be traumatized for life. Be especially aware of the signs and anticipate them. Safety and calmness are often critical in this situation.

A horse has conscious input with flight and fight, and will choose his action depending on the event and the context. Freeze and faint responses are far more unconsciously directed. In our experience, these responses also correspond to certain breeds or types. For example, cold-blooded horses may sometimes seem calm, yet they can be "frozen" with fear. One way to study your own horse is to ride with a heart-rate monitor. Many horses that are afraid will have a high heart rate, even though their behavior seems normal.

## Body Language

The freestyle groundwork method provides additional information about a horse's temperament, human body language, and communication between people and horses. It provides a wealth of information to beginner riders, who have yet to discover exactly how the hierarchical relationship with their horse works. This method can reveal partnerships where the rider is not completely in charge. This type of relationship may be concealed when riding but not in work on the ground. Furthermore, groundwork offers significant advantages for riders who have not yet developed an independent seat. It is easier to learn to control your body language from the ground than in the saddle, and this method allows you to learn to train your horse without interference from your seat.

Communicating with horses is largely dependent on body language. People have the advantage of being able to learn how to adapt their body language. Though we can never match the horse's body language, we can certainly approximate it. In any case, we must learn to use our body

To understand a prey animal well, we need to know the survival techniques we may have to deal with in the course of training. "The Four Fs" stand for the order of the phases in which horses react when frightened: Flight, Fight, Freeze, and Faint. A good rider ensures he never reaches Phase 2 (fight)—let alone the following phases—because the rider will always lose. Phase 1 is sometimes permissible in training, provided the rider maintains control. We call this "guided flight."

language consciously. When doing freestyle groundwork or longeing, our body language includes our position, posture, and movement. With position, we change our angle to the horse (see the diagram below). When the trainer is a bit behind the horse he is in the driving circle of the horse and he encourages the horse to go forward. When the trainer changes his position by going a bit more forward into the leading circle he can make the horse slow down or stop.

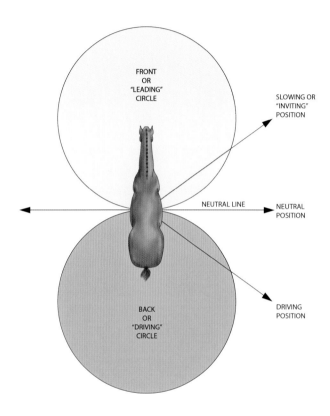

FRONT OR "LEADING" CIRCLE

SLOWING OR "INVITING" POSITION

NEUTRAL LINE

NEUTRAL POSITION

DRIVING POSITION

BACK OR "DRIVING" CIRCLE

With movement, the trainer can move toward or away from the horse. This influences the horse's speed. Moving forward toward him makes the horse go faster; moving passively backward away from him slows the horse down. By moving away from the horse in the leading circle, we can ask the horse follow us.

With our posture, we can be "driving," "slowing and inviting," or "neutral." Driving involves action and energy, slowing and inviting is relaxed, soft, and creates space between you and the horse, and neutral is active but relaxed. With the slowing and inviting posture, combined with moving away from the horse, you can "invite" the horse to follow you. When doing this, you can both walk forward and backward, as long as you move away from the horse. This is what we see during demonstrations by Emiel Voest, and by horseman like Monty Roberts, when he realizes Join-Up®. This is typical behavior of a herd animal that likes to follow—"be lead by"—a higher ranking animal (or a human being).

*In order to fine tune communication during freestyle groundwork or longeing, you must first imagine two circles drawn around the horse—as seen here. The driving circle is located around the horse's hindquarters: when you step into this circle, it is to encourage the horse to go forward or faster. When you move sideways a few steps into the leading circle, the horse will stop or turn around ("slowing" position), and from this position you can also ask the horse to follow you (leading position). When you want the horse's movement to remain unchanged, you stand in the neutral position in the middle just between the two circles.*

*We like to say that horses with different temperaments have "different-size" circles: for example, a horse that easily goes forward has a large driving circle area. This type of horse has a forward drive and goes faster during freestyle groundwork when the trainer steps forward into his (big) driving circle. For a horse with a "small" driving circle, the trainer has to make more steps forward to get closer to the horse and has to spend much more driving energy to make him go forward. These experiences with work on the ground are mostly the same as when riding. But with this freestyle work, we are able to test the forward drive of our young horses and also their willingness to follow us, in other words, to be led.*

*In a Dutch research project (Horsonality, 2002, by researcher Ir. Kathalijne Visser) three key points of the personality of horses were investigated: temperament and emotion; the ability to learn; and the willingness to cooperate (to be led). We are convinced that we get a lot of extra information on these essential aspects from freestyle groundwork and longeing. It is a good way to look at your horse and study his personality. We consider the observation and study of the personality of our horses to be an extremely important aspect of dressage at the highest level.*

Many people deal with body language from an unconscious-incompetence position (see p. 3). For instance, let's say you want to catch your horse in the field. Inexperienced people move toward the horse. When the horse walks away, they follow and try to catch him. Sometimes they even get angry, which is immediately translated into an "active" posture. Of course, this is totally counterproductive as they get the opposite of what they want because their intention and their body language do not match and the horse remains in the field!

We often do something incorrectly (incompetence), but we do not realize that we are doing it wrong (unconscious). This results in mutual incomprehension and subsequently leads to a total communication breakdown. Optimum body-language use depends on our ability to observe a horse's reactions and correctly translate them. In short, we have to ask ourselves: what does my horse mean by the way he behaves and reacts to my body language? If we want to communicate with our horses at the body language level, we must learn to make our intentions clear through our body language. Therefore, we must make visible distinctions in our position, movement, and posture. When we ride the horse we have different communication abilities, based on the same principles, but without the visible distinctions as when we are on the ground. The horse cannot see us; just feel us. This makes it even more difficult.

*Emiel's body language is neutral, he is relaxed but active and he is leaving the horse on his own. From this posture, he can immediately change to the driving or to the slowing and inviting position, if necessary. To make the horse go faster, Emiel would step into the driving circle, his position combined with his active posture makes the horse go faster (see photo on p.24).*

*To slow the horse down, Emiel steps into the leading circle. From there he is able to stop the horse and then "lead" him: that is, Emiel's posture will become relaxed, he'll move away from the horse, and the horse will follow (see photo on p. 27).*

Inviting a horse to follow involves creating space between you and the horse, combined with making yourself small, breathing from your diaphragm, and folding your hands in front of your body or letting them hang. You move forward away from the horse, or move backward.

Driving clearly involves more domination/action. You make yourself big and spread your arms and hands. You move actively, and move forward toward the horse.

## 1  Driving

Driving is distinguished by body positions and movements that require an energetic, "directive" to perform effectively. Although more activity is part of driving nothing should be seen as "aggressive" and certainly not cause flight. The movement of driving is forward, both in intention and direction.

*Associated words for driving include: active, big, more, open, forward, convincing, and square.*

## 2  Slowing and Inviting

With a slowing action, you ask the horse to go slower or stop. You do this by moving into his leading circle and a little bit away from him to make space between you. From slowing and then stopping him, you can invite him to follow you. In this context, the word "inviting" mainly means

*Tineke with her favorite Standard Poodle James. When you want to teach your dog to sit before you cross a street, you must reward him as he sits. Good timing is very important. If you reward your dog when he stands up again, you are rewarding him for the wrong action.*

creating space. You stay in the leading circle. Your movement should go in the desired direction. Therefore, an inviting posture position works better for making a horse follow you than an active one, although this does not mean there is no activity while leading a horse. "Small" is also a concept that goes with inviting: small in posture and movement. With respect to direction of movement, the trainer moving backward is inviting, or "leading." Backward movement may be in the form of walking or moving a hand.

*Several words to associate with inviting include: small, less, closed, backward, soft, and round.*

### 3 Neutral

Neutral is like the word "consolidate"; in other words, you want to leave the horse to do what he is already doing. The key word with neutral is relaxation, by which we mean an active relaxation, not a passive one. The second word that is important with neutral is middle or central. A neutral position is one between driving and leading, in which you stay ready to immediately start driving or leading. You act very calmly, moving neither forward nor backward; however, you ensure that the horse knows you are present and ready for action. A neutral position can still command respect.

*Associated words with neutral include: relaxation, middle, calmness, and alertness.*

## Clarity

Sometimes our bodies do not do what we want. As long as that is the case, you cannot be consistent in your use of body language. Furthermore, your body language will confuse your horse. As a result, your horse will not always approach you, even though you invite him to come. For example, you may intend to "call" your horse with an inviting motion, but instead, you inadvertently assume a driving posture, thus asking your horse to move away. The result is a very confused horse. You must develop consistent body language before you can communicate with your horse clearly.

Horses benefit from clarity. In this context, clarity is making things understandable for the horse. This means always doing the same action at the right moment—that is, being predictable and having the right timing. If your horse's reaction suggests that he does not understand you, then adjust the question or the aid so he can.

People often give very contradictory messages: we want one thing, but our body communicates something totally different. Driving the horse while moving backward does not work. You can experience the results of these opposing actions during a groundwork or longeing session. Asking your horse to come to you while using an active, big, "forward" posture

does not work either. You can also confuse the horse by talking to him in a calming voice while your body language communicates tension or aggression.

Some time ago, we observed a man who wanted to teach his dog to sit before crossing the street. The dog sat obediently for the man, but the man rewarded the dog exactly at the moment that he stood again. In other words, the man rewarded his dog for standing, not sitting. The dog will definitely not remain sitting the next time—and perhaps the man will not realize his mistake. Clarity leaves no room for doubt, uncertainty, and bad timing. Your horse can only understand what you ask of him if your voice and body express the same thing. As a trainer, you must be aware of the exercise you ask for and the technique you use.

Certainty automatically makes your posture more compelling, something to which horses are very sensitive. All top trainers demonstrate certainty in their body language. Major enemies of certainty are doubt and fear. Far too often, riders are actually afraid of their horse but still try to be the leader. Talk about contradictions!

*Emiel is demonstrating the "inviting" body language. His posture is relaxed, he moves away from the horse. The horse is following. From their herd instinct horses are programmed to follow "respected" leaders. You don't get this respect for free, you have to earn it!*

You do not get your horse's respect automatically, you have to earn it. The horse has to accept your leadership and learn to feel safe with you. Respect is about your acting with confidence, clarity, and consistency. Confidence automatically makes your posture more convincing. Major enemies of confidence are doubt and fear.

## Respect and Trust

Respect is a concept that clearly has two sides to it: one side is the horse's respect for the higher ranking leader; the other is the trainer's respect for the horse. Without respect for the horse, the rider will never gain the horse's respect. Do not misconstrue a horse's fear as respect for his rider! You do not get your horse's respect automatically; you have to earn it. Expanding your knowledge gives you more confidence, which automatically makes your posture more convincing.

In addition, clarity is very important. The horse should never suffer as a result of your questions or directions. A horse does not understand unjust or poorly timed punishment. This makes a horse afraid, and that is the point at which you lose his respect. Your ability to get a horse to relax and feel safe is precisely what makes him respect you.

Trust is the ultimate goal for which we all strive. You do not earn trust just liking your horse and caring for him well. Trust only comes when you can actually practice all the preceding concepts. You have to communicate on a level that he can understand. Your horse will only feel safe when you act clearly and with confidence. This is the foundation on which trust can grow. Understand, however, that trust is a fragile concept: unfortunately it takes less effort to break trust than to build it!

## Figure Out or Understand

People learn mainly by understanding and/or seeing the "sense" of something. Horses learn differently. They do not necessarily have to see the sense of an exercise as long as they understand what they are supposed to do, and, at the same time, associate that action with something positive (reward). In other words, a horse has to gain something that improves his situation by performing an action.

Emiel Voest frequently makes this distinction by using the words "figure out" and "understand." If a horse is led out of his stall 100 times, he will probably follow his handler 100 times. The horse figures out how he should respond to the handler's aids but does not understand why he should leave his stall 100 times. Fortunately for us, a horse apparently does not need to understand why something is; he only needs to figure out things enough to be useful to us.

This means that we have to learn how to think differently about training and not assume that a horse knows why a circle has to be round instead of oval. Every incorrectly ridden circle is incorrectly ridden by the rider and not incorrectly performed by the horse. There is always an Action (aid) from the rider and a Reaction (response) from the horse (for a full explanation of this technique: Action, Pressure, Reaction, and Reward, see Training with the Question and Answer Method, p. 77). A horse benefits when he is rewarded for a good reaction, in which case,

RIDE HORSES WITH AWARENESS AND FEEL

he will want to repeat it the next time.

Food can be a reward but so can rest. Rest should always be the first, and therefore, the most important reward when you are teaching a horse from the saddle. Rest comes in many forms, from you stopping the aid by relaxing your muscles or exhaling, to release leg or rein pressure, to a break from work.

## Timing

Research shows that a horse must be rewarded within a second of his correct reaction; otherwise, he does not make the connection between action, reaction, and reward, and the reward becomes ineffective. Ideally, we reward the horse the moment he responds. There is seldom any use in punishing or correcting a horse after an undesired behavior. Intervention before the undesired behavior (when you feel it coming on) is much more effective than correction afterward.

Punishing a horse—for example, by hitting him for biting—requires extremely careful timing to be effective at all. Many horses have been hit for years for biting, but they still continue to bite. The most effective moment for both reward and correction is the so-called motivation (or de-motivation) point. This point is after the horse has decided and a fraction of a second before he actually performs a specific act or makes a move. You can learn to recognize these moments through observation and experience. If you act at the right moment, you can make your point by doing very little. The following applies to correction: you achieve more with less.

## Giving Direction with Small Signals

The leader always has the control, which is something we have to contend with as riders. For many horse lovers, groundwork is a good training method for learning to gain this control. It teaches us quite quickly how easily we can communicate with a horse when we use his "language."

Horses need only a very small signal to alert them to perform a major response. They depend on this type of signal for survival in the social context of the herd and find it quite normal to respond immediately. As mentioned, horses are team players. They work together both out of necessity and natural willingness. The horse's social behavior is primarily oriented toward other horses, but fortunately, horses are not very choosy; there are many examples of horses exhibiting social behavior toward other species, such as dogs, goats, and even chickens and people!

Of course, general knowledge about body language is important, but bear in mind that individual preferences can make a big difference. To communicate with a horse, we must use the language our horse can un-

Horses need only very small signals to respond to major tasks. They depend on these signals for survival in the social context of the herd and find it quite normal to respond to them immediately. In this respect, horses are team players.

derstand. The training aids from the ground that Emiel Voest uses are position, movement, and posture; when we ride, we use our legs, hands, weight, and voice.

## Dealing with Reflexes

Many of the horse's daily actions are based on reflex, necessary for survival in the herd. However, reflexes as a result of fear can sometimes provoke the wrong outcome. We have already learned that frightened horses can suffer from a form of what we might call "restricted awareness," when they close themselves off from their surroundings and stop responding to aids that they would do well under normal conditions. As we've said, use of punishment to correct a horse in this state only exacerbates the fear so is completely useless (p. 21). Fear causes a horse to act "reflexively," meaning that he acts unconsciously—without thinking—(like the flight response, for example). And, a bolting horse does not feel his rider's aids anymore.

A reflexive behavior cannot be corrected; the solution to changing behavior lies before the act, not after it. Prevention is the best solution, and for things that we cannot escape in our dealings with horses, we need to get them accustomed to what they are afraid of step by step. This process requires a great deal of knowledge, experience, and unusually good timing on the part of the trainer! Key words in this situation include: clarity, relaxation, calmness, safety, and patience.

*Fear-based reflexes must be counterbalanced by learned actions. In this photo, Emiel Voest is working with our Prix St. Georges horse Nurejev to overcome his fear of applause. He got Nurejev accustomed to the noise of the crowd and rewarded him when he acted courageously. The audience applauded only at Emiel's direction, who took on the role of "conductor." He instructed them to clap, clap louder, clap softer, and stay quiet.*

RIDE HORSES WITH AWARENESS AND FEEL

One of our horses had a fear reflex to applause. The sound made him totally crazy: he would try to flee or lie down and would not respond to his rider. After Horse Event (a show at the Academy) in 2001, Tineke and Imke started giving clinics with Emiel Voest. During one of these clinics, our horse spooked when he heard the applause. Emiel immediately incorporated that into the clinic. He instructed the audience to clap and cheer louder or softer, depending on his hand signals. When the horse took off, the audience kept applauding. Emiel applied pressure on the horse's halter with a lead rope. As soon as the horse took a step toward the audience, Emiel immediately lightened this pressure and the audience applauded more softly. In this way, the horse was rewarded for his courage. After three times, the horse's fear had clearly diminished. The applause became manageable for him and therefore less frightening. To sum up, the moment the horse stopped running away, Emiel recognized the Target Behavior (see p. 88) and immediately rewarded the horse for it (timing). This is one of the ways in which Emiel, as well as world-renowned trainers such as Monty Roberts, train their horses.

Combining impressions, (positive association) is also used a great deal in circus training. Trainer Marjolein Kylstra of Showstal Penthesileia in Rhenen accustoms her horses to applause by making a lot of noise with a rattle while feeding them. As a result, something frightening becomes associated with something pleasant. This concept can also be applied to other situations, including loading a horse in a trailer and getting him to walk by a frightening object. This is the time-honored principle of police-horse training. When a horse is afraid of something, you do not avoid the situation; on the contrary, you find a scary situation and connect it with something pleasant to create a positive association.

## Reaction Follows Action

It is no surprise that flight animals have a very high reaction speed—they sense an environmental stimulus (the Action) and respond to it (Reaction). The result is that the action and the reaction are always immediately connected—a horse never reacts later on; he always reacts "now."

You can unintentionally teach a horse to respond incorrectly by rewarding him at the wrong moment. The example given earlier in this chapter of the man with the dog illustrates this principle. If the man does not reward the dog immediately when he sits but rewards him when he stands again, the dog will not stay sitting down the next time. The reward comes too late and has the opposite effect. This results in a reaction that has to be corrected; the dog first has to unlearn what the man taught him. This takes twice the effort.

The same principle applies to training horses. Remember that horses take flight when they do not understand an aid or find it frightening! This is why they often run off or come off the aids when they are learning a difficult movement, such as flying changes. Our mare Sunrise was an example. She was so afraid of flying changes that just riding her on the diagonal would make her run off in panic. Such behavior often occurs when the gap between what a horse knows and what the rider wants is too big. Sunrise may have had a bad experience before we got her. It took almost two years before Tineke, with her endless patience, got Sunrise to relax in her changes. Fortunately, we can say that it worked out well. So, the message is: do everything right the first time!

An exercise must be broken down into many small interim steps, and all these steps have to be learned one by one. A rider that asks the horse to take too big a step invites incomprehension, confusion, or even anger. As a result, the rider—unaware and again unintentionally—trains the horse to use his flight reflex, which is unfortunate because the rider will later have to teach the horse not to run away. Riding a horse that takes off in response to his flight reflex is unsafe and unpleasant. Preventing this response is very important. This means that we must learn to recognize the small signs that precede the flight position. Intervention is considerably easier when we can act early. In practical terms, this means diffusing tension upon seeing the smallest signs of it rather than allowing the horse to build up more tension, in which case you are always too late.

## Yield to Pressure

Emiel Voest regularly uses the concept of the horse yielding to pressure in his system. We think this is very important. Actually, every rider uses yielding to pressure as a training method. Consider that you ask the horse to yield to the bit or move sideways from the pressure of one calf.

The problem with yielding to pressure lies in the fact that horses, by nature, move into or against the pressure, certainly when pressure is used without subtlety. Every horse responds to being girthed by pushing his barrel against the tightening of the girth. Pulling on a lead rope also elicits an opposite reaction: a horse does not drop his head but raises it reflexively. These examples illustrate the reverse reflex phenomenon. The word "reflex" says it all: the reaction is a reflex, that is, an unconscious action, and the horse does not think about it. The most important implication of this fact is that we should never correct or punish this reaction. What we must do is teach a horse to respond with a conscious reaction in place of an unconscious one, which in this case, is yielding to pressure and not pushing into it.

Another example of an "incorrect" reflex is a horse that keeps bumping his head when he's being loaded into a trailer or when entering a stall with a low door. Mexican, the horse on which Imke won the individual bronze medal and the team gold at the Young Riders European Championship in Helsinki, was seriously injured several times this way. He constantly bumped his head when he had to pass underneath something.

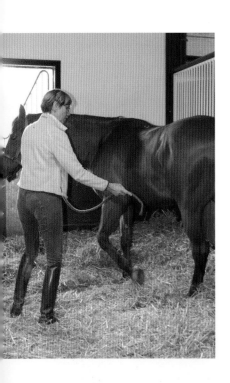

*A horse must learn to move away from—or yield to—pressure. For this purpose, you must teach your horse a conscious reaction to replace the unconscious reflex, which is to move "into" or "against" pressure. In this photo, Tineke asks a horse to move away from her in the stall. Training starts here. Actually, the horse's reaction is the same as yielding to the leg under saddle.*

As an emergency solution, we finally used a standing martingale to hold his head down whenever we transported him. We never did succeed in getting rid of this "incorrect" reflex and had to continue using the martingale. But a solution like this just treats the symptoms. It is much better to take the time to teach a young horse how to yield to pressure in the first place.

## Conclusion

To understand the horse really well, you need to deepen your knowledge of typical prey animal traits and the flight reaction. Fortunately, the horse is also a herd animal (like we are), which explains their affinity for hierarchy and cooperation. As we've said, the horse likes to be part of a team. People can make use of these traits, provided they learn how to control and suppress their human "predatory" qualities. Dealing with the horse—a prey animal—requires understanding, respect, consistency, and body-language control. You'll only get respect when you project leadership.

Horses use body language to communicate with one another. So, your postures and gestures are more meaningful than your voice; become aware of your body language and learn how to control it. The groundwork method is a good way to practice this. Only when you can be consistently clear with your body language—even in the stall and while grooming—can you expect a horse to understand what you want. Remember, a horse ultimately only needs very small signals in order to understand you.

Moving into or against pressure is usually a reflexive act: a horse will raise his head reflexively when someone pulls on his lead rope. Our training is based on teaching a horse the opposite: yielding or "giving" to pressure. As examples, consider how a horse yields to pressure from the bit or moves laterally from the pressure of your leg.

*Imke talks with Emiel about Sunrise. Academy riders always study their horses' personality. The freestyle groundwork training system can also be useful in this regard as it provides you another way to observe a horse. When we first started training Sunrise, this really helped us understand that we needed to be a bit stricter with our dominant alpha mare. Once we reversed the "ranking" hierarchy with her rider gradually becoming boss, Sunrise became very cooperative, and as affectionate as a lap dog.*

# Imke on Emiel Voest

I MET EMIEL VOEST in 2001 when we were discussing the plans for the first Horse Event in Deurne. Emiel wanted to put on a clinic using one of our Grand Prix horses. Tineke invited him to the Academy because we first wanted to see him work at our place. We thought he could repeat his work in Deurne, so we let Emiel borrow Barbria for his clinic.

With an audience of about 2,000 in Deurne's big indoor hall, Barbria followed Emiel like a lamb and she performed all the exercises we had bet she would refuse to do! We were truly dumbfounded. She had always been afraid to go by strange objects, her whole life. And she often tested my mother's patience—and mine, too. However, within a half hour, Emiel was leading her between jumps, getting her to walk on a sail, and—to top it all off—making her stand on a kind of plank that functioned like a teeter-totter. In a short space of time, she accepted Emiel as her natural leader and apparently found his position next to her on the ground much more reassuring than our position in the saddle. We talked about this experience for a long time. Would Barbria's training have progressed faster had we started by building her confidence from the ground to deal

with the things she found so frightening?

After that first Horse Event, we were so impressed by Emiel that we invited him back to the Academy. With my father and all the Academy staff present as the audience, we let Emiel try my current top horse Sunrise in the ring. The Smarius family, Sunrise's owners, had brought her to us a year earlier. Sunrise was tense, and her stride at the walk was bigger going to the left than to the right. Tineke rode her for a year, handling her with kid gloves. Nevertheless, Sunrise remained tense, resisted easily, and acted afraid when we wanted to teach her something new. As we've noted, the flying changes, in particular, were a big problem. When we would ask for a change, she would run away. We thought the problem was possibly due to some bad experiences she had before she came to our barn. Sunrise's progress was slow, even with Tineke's great patience and softness—her usual approach. We started to doubt that things would work out.

Emiel made Sunrise move off several times with the lead rope and worked her for 15 minutes. He concluded that she is extremely intelligent and has a good temperament. He thought her problems could be solved as her fears and frustrations did not seem

to be very deep-rooted. Tineke continued training Sunrise in good spirits. Several weeks later, Emiel was back at the Academy for the spring course, which sparked many interesting discussions. Anky van Grunsven was present, too. We told her about Emiel's approach, and she was quite interested. Emiel put Sunrise in the ring again, and then Tineke rode her.

An interesting conversation followed. Anky did not think Sunrise was afraid; she found the mare quite dominant and said: "I think she just wants to be the boss." We asked ourselves how domination and fear could look so much alike. Emiel explained that domination and fear often go hand in hand in nature: "The most fearful horse lives the longest." With Emiel's help, we determined that Sunrise was a typical "alpha mare" that resisted submitting to the leadership of her rider. She sometimes became angry when we asked her to do new things. She ran away or urinated in protest—not out of fear but out of domination.

Tineke had to make sure she was the leader and did not become distracted by all Sunrise's antics. There was just one solution: to train even more clearly, consistently, and a bit more strictly. Once Sun-

rise learned that Tineke was her leader, she totally blossomed; and after she accepted the new hierarchy, she proved to be very talented and very sweet.

In the fall of 2004, Tineke gave Sunrise to me as consolation for losing Lancet. At our first international show in the spring of 2005, we won the Freestyle at the big show in Wiesbaden; several months later, we won our second international show in Hickstead. In the winter, we had one success after another in the World Cup. In March 2006 at the Indoor Brabant show, I beat my personal best in the Freestyle, scoring approximately 80%, and in the World Cup Final in Amsterdam, I achieved my best international performance. I had placed seventh and sixth in the final on Barbria, but I now placed fifth on Sunrise! Anky was right: Sunrise turned into a dream horse, once she became submissive.

Since then—with Emiel's guidance—I have worked other horses with the help of groundwork. The experience provides added information about a horse's personality and is very valuable. In addition, you learn to understand from the ground—instead of from the saddle—how communication works with a horse using the Question and Answer Method (p. 77).

*Positioning and bending are essential gymnastic exercises. In this photo, Imke is riding Sunrise in shoulder-in, an exercise on three tracks, in which the right front leg and the left hind leg move on the same track. Imke continually changes the bend. She also regularly rides with positioning and no bend; in other words, the horse's legs track in the usual manner (stay on the track), but the horse is positioned to the inside or outside. Be sure that the horse is always equal on both reins and does not learn to fall out over the shoulder.*

## CHAPTER 3
# Self-Knowledge and Self-Control

### Your Conscious Mind and Your Subconscious Body

Sometimes your body does not do what you want. For example, you want your legs to hang quietly on the horse's sides, but your instructor tells you that your legs are still clamped, "banging" on the horse's sides. You feel as if your body is resisting you and that it is evidently being controlled by something other than your conscious mind. This is because, in addition to your conscious, you have a subconscious mind, too.

Dutch sports analyst Freek de Jonge once wrote: "This is what soccer is like: when you take a penalty kick, your subconscious is screaming: 'Stop!' and then you miss the opportunity to score. As long as your subconscious mind is the boss, you will fail: when your conscious mind cannot silence your subconscious, you will not be able to get the ball into the top corner of the goal." (For more on this theory and why the subconscious overrules the conscious, see "No" Does Not Exist on p. 47.)

The same goes with riding horses. It is a mental game. Learning to ride involves aligning your subconscious body with the wishes of your conscious mind. The subconscious surrenders itself only with constant training and repetition. You are a good rider when your body performs what your mind asks of it and when the body and mind are joined in balance.

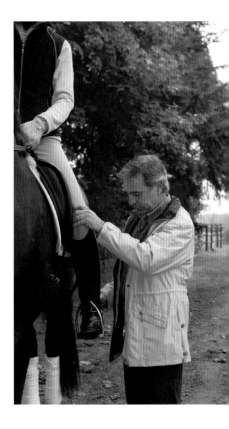

*Richard Weis checks to see if Imke's upper legs, lower legs, and feet are relaxed. Our body sometimes does not do what we want. For example, you try to let your legs hang quietly on your horse's sides, but your instructor says they are still moving too much. Your "unconscious" body can only learn to listen to your "conscious" mind with a great deal of training (going from unconscious-incompetence to conscious-competence, see p. 41).*

### Look in the Mirror

Equestrian sports demand physical and mental control. You are not working with a ball, bicycle, or stick but with a living animal. You have to adapt to the animal, and this can only happen when you start with the specific traits and qualities of that animal. You can only communicate what you want from your horse if you know exactly what you want to achieve and how you want to achieve it, and this only works when you can control your body and your mind. Riders must go through an intensive learning process in order to adequately gain this control.

Many riders sit on a horse without the necessary knowledge, control, and technique. This is why we at the Academy focus a great deal of

**Your body is evidently controlled by something other than your conscious will. Learning to ride horses is about aligning the subconscious body with the wishes of the conscious mind. The subconscious "surrenders" control only with constant repetition. You are a good rider when your body performs what your mind asks of it—that is, when the body and mind are joined in balance.**

attention on the mental processes necessary for riders to develop themselves. The most important part of this is to know oneself well. A rider should "look in the mirror" regularly with the help of an instructor (if needed), set clear goals, and know how to improve himself.

The world of equestrian sports generally invests more in horse training than in rider training. This is not effective. Nine out of 10 riding mistakes are made by the rider. A top rider with a somewhat less talented horse will generally perform better than a less skilled rider with a top horse. Therefore, more attention should be paid to training and supporting the rider.

## The Automatic Pilot

Our internal "computer" is like an iceberg: only the tip is visible above water. This tip is the conscious part of the computer; however, a much larger part—the subconscious—of which we are not aware, is under water.

*A human's "internal computer" is like an iceberg: most of it is under water, and most of your actions are done subconsciously. When these actions go well, you hardly think about them; you are in a kind of trance. In professional jargon, this state is called "flow." Imke experienced flow in Athens. After her test, she said, "I didn't have to do anything; Lancet did it all himself." It does not get any better than that!*

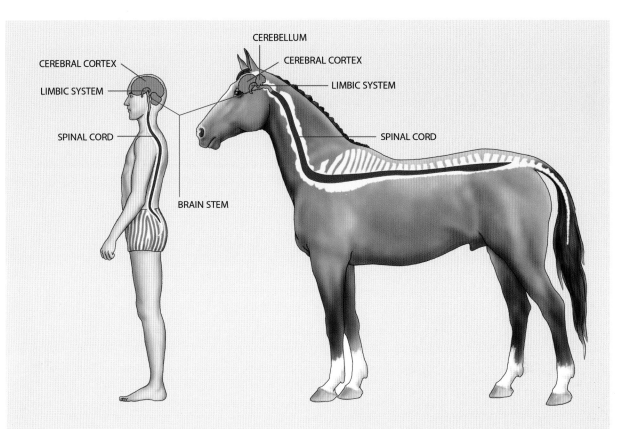

CEREBELLUM

CEREBRAL CORTEX

CEREBRAL CORTEX

LIMBIC SYSTEM

LIMBIC SYSTEM

SPINAL CORD

SPINAL CORD

BRAIN STEM

The brain consists of three main parts: the brain stem (green), the limbic system (red), and the cerebral cortex. The brain has developed over the course of evolution as follows: first the brain stem, then the cerebellum, and later the cerebral cortex. Certain reptiles only have a brain stem; higher developed animals also have a cerebellum; and mammals have a brain stem, cerebellum, and cerebral cortex. The human cerebral cortex is clearly larger than that of the horse. The higher mental functions of the human brain are located in the neocortex.

The green colored brain stem is also called the *reptilian brain*. Those in the fields of psychology and typology assert that this is where intuition is located. Emotion is contained in the red areas, and reason is situated in the blue areas.

People are proud of their unique ability to reason, so they often think they can achieve everything with reason. However, in sports, people discover that their unconscious body does not always listen to their conscious will. Likewise, horse enthusiasts tend to assume that horses also can

reason or think logically. But they cannot.

Incidentally, people, by definition, are not *all* logical because they still have those parts of the brain depicted in green and red. In principle, even people are a "chunk" of emotion.

Any person can be dominant in a particular color. You can use a test to determine your preferred color. The Structogram® is such a test and a tool to help determine the dominant parts of the brain in a person, according to the color scheme illustrated in this diagram. Sports psychologist Rico Schuijers says that, from an evolutionary perspective, horses are primarily red, according to the Structogram® theory. He thinks that riders who test very blue—dominant riders—are quicker to experience communication problems with their horses than people who are dominant in other colors. Riders who test very green can adapt well to their horse but tend not to provide enough leadership. Finally, riders who test very red are probably very "show-oriented." They should take care that they do not demand too much from their horse or themselves.

When this subconscious part works for you, everything is fine; however, when it works against you, you have to take action. You must try to teach the subconscious to learn to listen to the conscious part so that you can change it. What we mean by the subconscious (or unconscious) is not the deepest part of the brain but something very practical, what you need almost every minute of your life, such as breathing or blinking your eyes.

Modern psychology uses the concept "adaptive unconsciousness"; this means that we need that part of the subconscious that churns out data like a giant internal computer in order to survive. This process largely takes place without your knowledge, but you use it constantly. If you walk down the street and a car suddenly comes directly at you, you react before you think about all the possibilities. You do not have time to think if you should move left or right. You can only survive by jumping out of the way quickly without thinking about it.

We call this part of our "computer" the automatic pilot. This automatic pilot helps you thousands of times each day. Sometimes your automatic pilot has already made a decision while you are still mulling over the right reaction. We are raised to refrain from making rash decisions. We do not like to navigate blindly on our automatic pilot. Even our language is full of sayings that encourage us to exercise caution, such as "haste makes waste" and "look before you leap." We prefer to gather a lot of information and deliberate and think about it a long time. We do not like to act fast.

However, riding horses depends on fast decisions, which are the result of our internal "computer" processing millions of bits of stored data at lightning-quick speed. We need to learn to trust our automatic pilot to become good riders, and therefore, we have to train hard and acquire a great deal of experience.

### Rider "Feel" and Automatic Pilot

When riding, your body learns how to respond to certain stimuli from the horse. This often happens without your knowledge. You ride, in part, on automatic pilot. Some top riders can hardly explain what they do; they just do it. They have developed "rider feel." But what actually is this? Rider feel is based on the experiences stored in our memories. Many experiences are captured in the so-called "cell memories" of the muscles and the spinal cord, unconsciously—without your knowledge.

Although it is interesting and educational to evaluate this process on occasion, it is also good to know that you do not have to explain everything; constantly looking for a reason can be a hindrance. Although tennis coach Vic Braden became frustrated because he could not find a rational explanation for his talent for predicting double faults, this did not diminish the quality of his talent.

Many riders have trouble engaging their automatic pilot. Do you know the feeling, too? This is the force that compels you to think constantly and give yourself orders, like "outside leg, inside rein, heels down…" This kind of thinking sometimes gets in the way, which is why you should sometimes just stop thinking and clear your mind!

## Good Riding Is "Unconscious-Competence"

We use a teaching model at the Academy that is based on the following four stages of performance:

*1 Unconscious-incompetence:* You actually cannot ride at all, but you do not yet know this.
*2 Conscious-incompetence:* In this stage, you realize that you cannot yet ride well. You are conscious of your lack of competence.
*3 Conscious-competence:* You can ride quite well but not automatically. You have to give a great deal of thought to the act of riding.
*4 Unconscious-competence:* You ride into the dressage arena without thinking about it. You are focused only on your horse. Riding is almost automatic. It is as though everything happens naturally. Your automatic pilot has taken over.

Hundreds of riders over the past years have been introduced to this learning model at the Academy. They have learned that training usually happens in Stages 2 and 3. They have also learned that great riding and a world-class performance in the show ring almost always happens in Stage 4. It is more or less done unconsciously, on automatic pilot. How exactly does this work? Here is an example:

### 1 Unconscious-Incompetence
Imagine that you just finished your first riding lesson and quickly learned how to do rising trot on the correct diagonal. You feel great. Everything is going wonderfully riding your obedient school horse. You are already dreaming of a career like Anky van Grunsven's. You still do not know how long the road to the top is. You are not aware of the difficulties.

### 2 Conscious-Incompetence
You now have your own young horse, and you have fallen off him. Riding is not as easy as you first thought back when you only rode a well-broke school horse. You now know that you still have a lot to learn. This is a big step forward. At least you now know that riding is not a piece of cake. You experience step by step all the things you still have to learn.

### 3 Conscious-Competence
You are competing in your first dressage shows, and things are starting to go well. Your tests are good when everything comes together. Support

*Peter Murphy, technical advisor of the NOC\*NSF (sports website) and author of the book Totaal Coachen, is the driving force behind the use of sports psychology in equestrian sports. Pictured are Peter (with cap) and Imke talking in the stands of the dressage stadium at the Athens Olympics. Among the things we learned from Peter is the concept unconscious-competence. He is a major proponent of using a personality-based system in training and coaching. Murphy uses the Action Type system, which he and several colleagues developed based on the Myers-Briggs Type Indicator®.*

Winning show riders function at the unconscious-competence level. They are not occupied with other thoughts, such as exactly what to do to ride a movement, how their ride went yesterday, or what scores they will get. They ride in the here and now.

from your instructor is very important to you. You must concentrate in order to avoid making mistakes in your test because if you do not, things immediately do not go as well.

### 4 Unconscious-Competence

You now ride on automatic pilot. You have learned your test from memory so well that you no longer have to think about it. You dare to trust your reflexes. You automatically deal with the important things, like your horse's rhythm and the feeling he gives you. You are not distracted by other thoughts, such as exactly what you have to do to ride a movement, how your ride went yesterday, or what scores you will get from a judge. This is the stage in which riders achieve their victories. If things go really well, you feel like they almost happen automatically. You ride in a trance-like state. There is a word for this: flow. This is the ideal state for performing and is characterized by total concentration in which the athlete is sharp yet relaxed.

## Concentration Overcomes You

Concentration is a state of consciousness in which you are constantly aware of what you are doing and consequently, you are able quickly to direct your actions in the most precise way. You cannot just call up concentration; you can only create the conditions in which it can exist. Concentration can best be compared to sleeping. For example, when you want to go to sleep, you first do some preparing: you darken a room, shut out any noise, set the alarm clock, lie down, close your eyes, and then do nothing. When all this is done, you should fall asleep. The same process applies to concentration. But only *you* can create the necessary

*Imke celebrates after her ride at Indoor Brabant in 2006. This is the moment when an athlete comes "out of concentration." Her attention goes from "inside to outside," as it were, shifting from her horse to the spectators. This may happen after the final halt and salute. There are many things at a major international show that can cause you to lose concentration. You need to create the "conditions" so you can concentrate completely (see p. 44) and focus your full attention on the actions that are important at that moment and over which you have control.*

preparations conducive to be able to concentrate. We will discuss these in detail later, but first, we'll talk about the different characteristics of concentration, presented below in order: 1) passive; 2) here and now; 3) absolute; 4) individual differences.

### 1 Concentration Is Passive

Concentration, like sleep, just overcomes you. *Actively* wanting to sleep does not work; for example, it does no good to say "I have to sleep now." Likewise, saying "I have to concentrate" is just as ineffective. However, you can create the conditions for concentration so that you do not totally have to rely on chance.

### 2 Concentration Happens in the Here and Now

When a successful athlete is concentrating he is conscious of what is taking place at that moment. He focuses totally on the here and now. This means that he does not think about what he has just done and critique it. Doing so would be a hindrance during the competition because an athlete can only "judge" himself when he becomes his own "spectator." In contrast, an athlete should judge his performance during training when he has time to analyze it and improve himself. In competition, it is important to stay in the here and now. You must just perform the movements and trust that they are correct, instead of trying to control them. Control comes at the expense of the movement itself.

### 3 Concentration Is Absolute

You cannot concentrate less or more. Compare concentration to a light switch: a light is either on or off. The same applies to concentration: you are either concentrating or you are not. Lack of concentration does not mean you will perform poorly; however, you will not perform at a world class level.

### 4 Concentration and Individual Differences

As previously mentioned, concentration is about how quickly you observe situations and make subsequent actions. It can be different for athletes, though. For example, athletes in competitive sports may lose to opponents whose play is faster than theirs. They lose concentration while trying to keep up the pace, and consequently make mistakes.

## Attention and Automatism

As stated earlier, certain preparations must be made to achieve concentration. These are attention and automatism. An athlete must learn to direct and keep his attention entirely on his performance. He trains a number of hours a week to master skills, which include striving to make movement and combinations of movements automatic. We referred to this previously as being on automatic pilot. When he has achieved this, he is able to fully concentrate on the task at hand during a performance or competition.

## Concentration Circles

You can learn to concentrate. It begins with understanding how something works. Concentration requires you to deal with the here and now. The innermost circle (Circle 1) in the drawing on p. 44 represents ideal concentration where you are totally focused on everything that is important for riding well. You have no other thoughts and therefore are 100 percent occupied with "Me and my task," that is, riding. From this ideal place, however, you can be moved to Circle 2 because of distractions in your immediate surroundings, such as spectators opening their umbrellas as it starts to rain, or the judge's papers rustling in the wind. What should you do? Act as though nothing is happening? The answer is that you may look to see what is happening, but only if you quickly return to your state of concentration in Circle 1: "Me and my task."

Unfortunately, this does not always work. A horse that spooks at umbrellas can sometimes invite thinking like, "Oh no, he was so nice in the warm-up, and now he's terrible." Such thoughts are the beginning of the end—not relevant to the task at hand and therefore not helpful. You do not benefit by comparing what your horse was like earlier to what he is now. It is wasted energy to think about such things. You must focus only on those matters over which you now have control. Of course, this is easier said than done! Before you know it, you are in Circle 4 and think:

*Imke rides Lancet around the dressage ring in Athens, a few seconds before her test. This is the time for Imke and her horse to look at everything and get used to the surroundings. You can quietly let your horse look at objects that may disturb him. For example, if your horse is afraid of the judge's stands, go near them and try to reassure him. Imke gets Lancet to concentrate on her by riding tempo changes.*

"Oh, a mistake, now I'm going to lose!" And in Circle 5: "If I lose, then everybody at the barn will laugh at me." And, who has not found themselves in Circle 6: "What am I doing here?"

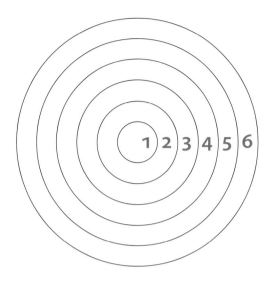

1   Me and my task
2   Direct distractions
3   "Should" comparison ("My horse does well in training, why not now?")
4   Winning and losing ("Oh, a mistake, now I'll lose!")
5   Consequences of winning and losing ("If I win/ lose, then…")
6   Questioning sense ("What am I doing here?")

## Concentration Is Different for Everyone

Athletes have different ways of preparing for competition. As said earlier, what works for one, does not work for another. Anky van Grunsven prepares for a test by being alone. She reads a book and listens to music, and in this way, goes into a kind of dream state. She crawls, so to speak, into a "tunnel" and does not see anything around her once she gets on her horse.

This strategy does not work for Anky's student Edward Gal. He discovered he did better by staying by the warm-up area and talking with his fellow competitors. All riders need to discover what works best for them. Here is a good tip: your preparation is often the opposite of your personality. A person who is introverted and has a lot of internal dialog—holding a mental conversation with himself—will not achieve concentration by withdrawing but by talking to others. On the other hand, an extroverted person, who normally tends to be easily distracted, may benefit more from an introverted type of preparation, such as listening to music on a headset.

Preparation also has to do with controlling the amount of tension the rider needs in order to compete. If you become tense easily, try to remain calm by practicing diaphragmatic breathing, for example. Some riders, though, need a little tension added in order to concentrate well. Tineke is such an example. She almost always rode her best tests when the grooms and trainers around her at the Olympic finals or other big shows had butterflies in their stomachs and transmitted their nervousness to her. She needed that "kick" to get the best out of herself. The right preparation for you can only be discovered in practice. A good dose of self-knowledge can help in this quest.

*Sports psychology has gained popularity in equestrian sports, particularly as a result of Anky's press conference after her gold medal win at the Sydney Olympics, when she explained that Peter Murphy's mental coaching was also responsible for her win. His coaching helped her analyze her mistakes in her first test. During that test, she had been focused on the wrong goal: "winning." When she later concentrated on "riding well," everything suddenly went better. She also benefited from her sports psychology knowledge in Athens, shown here. After a weak first ride, she had little trouble putting herself back into the right mental attitude. "Riding well and having fun" resulted in her second gold medal.*

## "No" Does Not Exist

We have stated that you should concentrate on "Me and my task" at shows and should not think about things over which you have no influence. When Anky thought about the gold medal during her first test at the Sydney Olympics, things went wrong. She mistakenly concentrated on something over which she had no control. But how do you do that— that is, not think about something? Because when you do not want to think about something, then you usually do!

At the Academy, we have an assignment we give to students. We tell them "Do not think about an orange." Almost immediately, they start laughing because they are all thinking about oranges and cannot help but do so. This demonstrates an important principle: your subconscious mind is incapable of understanding the difference between positive and negative, and consequently the word "no" does not exist. So if you keep saying to yourself: "I must not make any mistakes," your subconscious just hears the word "mistakes," and of course, then you will make a mistake. So try something else. Don't think about the orange; instead, think about a banana. When you are concerned about mistakes in your flying changes, don't think about them but concentrate instead fully on your horse's rhythm. For example, count canter strides on the diagonal and do the change on the same count every time. This helps a lot.

When Anky rode her second test in Sydney, she concentrated completely on having fun. She just wanted to have an enjoyable experience and she was not concerned anymore about making mistakes or not winning a medal. She had fun, and things also went well. Try this same approach. Concentrate on your horse's rhythm and nothing else. Or, focus totally on your breathing. Try diaphragmatic breathing. (It is a skill that has to be learned. Practice it lying down on a bed. Place your hands on your stomach. You will feel if you are breathing this way when you are relaxed.) Also, try to think only about positive things and keep them in your head. You will notice at first that you keep returning to other thoughts. Eventually, however, you will slowly but surely succeed in thinking for longer periods of good things about your horse's rhythm, or your diaphragmatic breathing.

## Motivation

Why do you ride? What is your motive? Have you ever asked yourself where this comes from? Although motivation to do something cannot be trained, it is still important to consider the origin of your desire. Answer the question honestly and discuss your answer with a good friend or a family member. It often requires a great deal of effort to establish what your true motives are for riding.

You need to learn to replace negative thoughts with positive ones. If you only say to yourself: "I must NOT make a mistake," then you will make it—often. If you do not want to make an error in the flying changes during a test, then you should not concentrate on the changes but on something else, such as your horse's rhythm or your own breathing.

*Sports psychologist Rico Schuijers recommends that we always engage in sports with a positive mind-set.*

*1 You continually want to improve yourself.*
Your motive for riding is task-oriented. Training and your own progress are more important than showing.

*2 You want to have fun.*
Your motive is non task-oriented. You do not have a need to continually become better, but you enjoy caring for your horse and having fun with him at home.

*3 You always want to win.*
It does not matter how you win, as long as you win. You like to enter shows where you can succeed, and you envision yourself standing on the highest step of the winner's podium. This stems from an ego-strengthening motivation.

*4 You do not want to lose.*
You look for shows with a weak field of competitors instead of shows where you know the competition is stronger. You worry primarily about being beaten, or you fear failure. This is ego-protecting motivation.

Ask yourself honestly what your strongest motives are. If you are truly non task-oriented, ask yourself whether you should really try to become a serious show competitor.

If you are task-oriented (1) and ego-protecting (4), you are probably a training fanatic who expects too much from yourself. A competitive rider benefits when his motives are task-oriented (1) and ego-strengthening (3).

But despite all these different reasons, ultimately, enjoyment of riding is the best motivator—even world-class riders find this goal the most important source of inspiration!

## Setting Goals

Each type of motivation requires a different goal. What kind of goals are there? And do you recognize these goals as ones you have?

*1 Result Goal*
You view your result in comparison with others. Who placed ahead of you and who placed behind you?

*2 Performance Goal*
You compare your performance with your previous ones to see if they have progressively improved. Your scores to date have been less than 62 percent. Did you score higher this time?

*3 Process Goal*
How did you achieve your performance? How did your training progress?

It is very important for every rider to set goals, but it is even more important to set goals that are within one's control. Such a goal, for

*Riding in the Olympics was a dream goal for Imke, which she hardly wanted to think about. That is why it was a surprise when she achieved her goal. The day before she left for Athens, Imke, who had been second reserve, was selected for the team. Her goal then became "get some experience and have fun." This is an ideal "process goal," certainly for someone like Imke, who is quite fanatical about the sport. In this case, there is no use in putting oneself under pressure with performance goals—for example: "I have to win"—as these only work negatively. It makes much more sense to avoid this level of pressure and set reasonable goals, which will make you feel good when you achieve them.*

example, is showing at a higher level. You can also ask your instructor to tell you when you have achieved a specific goal, such as keeping your hands quiet or getting your horse quicker off your leg. If your motivation is very task-oriented, in other words, you think training is more important than showing, you should occasionally set a result goal. You are already fanatical enough about training, but now you should want to win. In contrast, those not very task-oriented tend to have process goals. These types of people see training as necessary to making progress.

*Tineke, pictured here riding Sunrise on the Academy's galloping track, often focuses on "process goals" when training horses and teaching students. This means that she does not always train for shows. Showing a lot or practicing tests a lot can hinder your training progress. Enjoying training is a typical process goal for Tineke. A nice gallop on the track may not directly be the ideal preparation for a show the coming weekend, but it is a good way for horse and rider to have some fun in their work. According to Tineke, enjoyment also ultimately results in the best show scores.*

Process goals are not aimed at results of competition, but at yourself. They tell you how you achieved your performance. You do not look at your score but at those things over which you have influence, such as the process goals that appear in the list on p. 51. It can be very useful to score yourself or ask your trainer to score you on points such as hands, seat, or concentration.

*Process Goals Scoring List Sample (You may choose your own subjects.)*

| 1 | Well ridden | 1 | 2 | 3 | 4 | 5 | Poorly ridden |
|---|---|---|---|---|---|---|---|
| 2 | Quiet hands | 1 | 2 | 3 | 4 | 5 | "Busy" hands |
| 3 | Quiet seat | 1 | 2 | 3 | 4 | 5 | "Busy" seat |
| 4 | Relaxed muscles | 1 | 2 | 3 | 4 | 5 | Tense muscles |
| 5 | Quick reaction to the leg | 1 | 2 | 3 | 4 | 5 | Slow reaction |
| 6 | Calm/quiet | 1 | 2 | 3 | 4 | 5 | Excited/"busy" |
| 7 | Little effort | 1 | 2 | 3 | 4 | 5 | Great effort |
| 8 | Much enjoyment | 1 | 2 | 3 | 4 | 5 | Little enjoyment |
| 9 | Automatic pilot | 1 | 2 | 3 | 4 | 5 | Mental effort |
| 10 | Full concentration | 1 | 2 | 3 | 4 | 5 | No concentration |

## Smart Goals

Many athletes have a dream goal. It is important to translate this dream goal into mid-range and short-term goals. You can formulate smart goals by asking yourself the following questions: What do you want to achieve next year? What do you want to achieve next month? And what do you want to achieve tomorrow? These are important questions for an athlete. List your goals:

*1 What is your dream goal?*

For example, you want to be as good as Anky. Some young girls ride with that dream goal in the back of their minds. If that goal is not translated into something achievable, such as "go from training level to first level dressage within six months," then you will be constantly disappointed. Also, although riding like Anky is a wonderful goal, it is one that comes true for almost no one. So it turns out to be very frustrating because you can't reach your goal. It makes more sense to set a mid-range goal that is within your reach on the way to your dream goal.

*2 How do you translate this to the near future—for instance, a year from now?*

You may just be starting to ride and your long-term goal is to become a national or international dressage rider. This means that your mid-range goal—a year from now—may be to ride in a schooling show. This is attainable and a satisfying goal when it is achieved.

*Rico Schuijers talks with Imke in the warm-up ring after her record-scoring freestyle (80.5 %) at Indoor Brabant in 2006. Schuijers always recommends that his athletes set "smart goals," which means, among other things, focusing on goals that are specifically meaningful to you but also attainable. Imke's goal at Indoor Brabant was "to ride well." She did not give any prior thought to her score; it simply happened.*

### 3 What does this mean for the short term—let's say, one month?

This means that in one month's time, you want to easily do rising trot on the correct diagonal and canter your horse. If these goals are achieved sooner than expected, then this is a bonus that motivates you even more.

### 4 What will you do tomorrow?

If you want to achieve your goal but need help from others, start looking tomorrow for a good riding school or competent instructor.

Be sure you do not focus on goals that are unattainable. The most common mistake is to want too much too soon or not adjusting a goal that is set too high or too low. In one of sports psychologist Rico Schuijers' courses, he asked us to determine if we had chosen the right goals for ourselves, based on the questions below. Read them to see if you have chosen the right goals. See if they are realistic.

## Five Questions: Are Your Personal Goals S.M.A.R.T.?

If we take the first letter of each of the below five points and put them together, they spell the word SMART. In other words, these are smart goals that allow you to make progress.

### 1 Are your goals Specific?

Is your goal meaningful? Does it inspire you personally? Let's say you want to ride in a schooling show or go for a trail ride by yourself. The specific goal must challenge you personally. You must have the desire to achieve it!

*Imke and Joep watch a horse being schooled, something they often do. However, Joep is rarely present at the warm-up ring when Imke is showing. The two have made this agreement: Imke needs someone there like Tineke who "holds her back" (with a calming effect) as opposed to someone with a "drive" like hers, like Joep. So Joep has to drastically change his role when at a show.*

### 2 Are your goals Measurable?

Can you control or measure your goal in terms of scores, by showing at a higher level, or by doing a difficult exercise correctly as determined by your instructor?

### 3 Are your goals Action-oriented?

Is achieving this goal entirely within your control? Or do you have no influence over it, for example, who the judges are at a show or the condition of the footing? You should not be concerned about things over which you have no control. This is a waste of energy.

### 4 Are your goals Realistic?

Is your goal attainable? Within your reach? Many young riders these days want to become just as good as one of the Olympic dressage riders. As already mentioned, this is probably not the most realistic of goals because almost no one can achieve it. Setting such a goal invites disappointment.

*5  Are your goals Time-bound?*

Is your goal set too far in the future? Have you set a time for achieving it? Besides setting mid-range goals ("I want to move up a level within six months"), you also need to plan what you want to achieve next week or tomorrow.

Determine for yourself what your goals are and if they meet these five points. See if they are ones that help you stay motivated. Training practically happens by itself when you achieve your goals on a regular basis. Remember, do not set the bar too high and plan your goals from day to day.

## Differences in Learning Styles

Have you ever wondered why you immediately understand one trainer but not another? A student and teacher have to "click." Sometimes this does not happen. People in other sports have determined why things do not always gel. It is because not everyone learns in the same way. To help people learn easily, we can use the following diagram of learning and training styles. The learning styles are represented on two axes: "doing" and "looking" on the horizontal axis, and "feeling" and "thinking" on the vertical axis. Perhaps you can use the four learning styles equally, or you may learn best using one or two specific learning styles.

Learning to set "smart goals" is one of the most used tools in the sport. Do not set the bar too high and plan your goals from day to day. Make it easy for yourself. Training is a lot of fun when you can achieve your short-term goals.

*Tineke's Master Coach training has taught her to ask her students many questions during their lessons. Questions and answers help facilitate understanding between trainer and athlete. This process provides the trainer insight into how best the rider learns, and this will vary from person to person and by activity. The four "pillars" of learning are feeling, looking, thinking, and doing.*

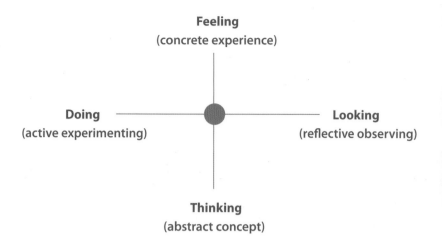

Feeling
(concrete experience)

Doing
(active experimenting)

Looking
(reflective observing)

Thinking
(abstract concept)

If you are a thinker, you first try to understand exactly how something should be carried out. Once you understand it, then you learn to apply it in practice. If you are a feeler, you learn best by practical experience. And a looker first has to see something before he can do it himself. A doer takes action and puts things into practice right away. Try to discover the easiest way for you to learn to ride.

## The Four Pillars of Learning

1  *Feeling: Learning by "Feel"*
   - You learn from specific experiences with horses.
   - You learn through relationships with people.
   - You are open to feelings and people.

2  *Looking: Learning by Looking and Listening*
   - You observe carefully before making judgment.
   - You view matters from different perspectives.
   - You look at the meaning of specific matters.

3  *Thinking: Learning by Thinking*
   - You learn by logically analyzing ideas.
   - You like to plan systematically and enjoy making notes.
   - You develop your action based on the intellectual concept of a situation.

4  *Doing: Learning by Doing*
   - You are capable of putting things together in practice.
   - You take risks easily.
   - You influence people and events by taking action yourself.

## Choose an Instructor Who Is a Good Fit

The way you learn best will work only when you find a compatible instructor. For example, if you are a rider who learns primarily by feeling and doing, you will have more difficulty learning from someone who is a thinking teacher. The thinker's detailed, theoretical explanation may go over your head. You hear the instructions, but you cannot to do anything with them.

Modern sports instructors have found a solution to this problem. They approach teaching from the student's perspective much more than was done in the past. They try to challenge their students and support them in their learning process—and let them make conscious choices. They are no longer just an instructor but someone who coaches according to the rider's needs.

Unfortunately, equestrian sports still do not have many teachers who practice this type of modern training. We are still more familiar with riding instructors who shout orders like a drill sergeant, an approach that stems from the military tradition of our sport of dressage. This tradition leads some to teach from an instructor-centered perspective rather than a student-centered one. If you do not click with your instructor, the only thing you can do is find one with whom you do.

*The Rabo Talent Plan was set up by the Academy and is run jointly with the KNHS (Royal Dutch Equestrian Sports Federation). It is based on the so-called Talent Guide, which consists of six success factors. These factors form the foundation on which top riders achieve their success. Pictured are some future "hopefuls," the 2006 Rabo Talent team from left to right starting in the back row: Huub van der Mark, Diederik van Silfhout, Piet Raymakers Jr, Jac Ansems, Dominique Filion, Lotje Schoots, Maikel van der Vleuten, Maikel van Mierlo, and Angela van den Berg.*

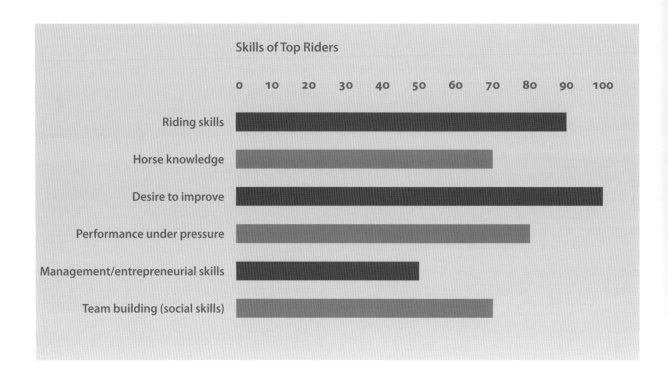

**Skills of Top Riders**

| | 0 | 10 | 20 | 30 | 40 | 50 | 60 | 70 | 80 | 90 | 100 |
|---|---|---|---|---|---|---|---|---|---|---|---|

- Riding skills
- Horse knowledge
- Desire to improve
- Performance under pressure
- Management/entrepreneurial skills
- Team building (social skills)

## Success in Riding

Success in riding depends on many different things. A rider may have talent, but not money and a good horse. Or, a rider may not be as accomplished, but he has a sponsor who provides him with good horses. The fact is, the less talented rider with access to several wonderful horses will have more success than the more talented one whose horses are not as good.

Several years ago, the Academy, along with the KNHS and HasKennistransfer developed the so-called Talent Guide: a list of six points that, according to world-class riders, influence whether or not one will have a successful career. The Talent Guide has become the starting point of the Rabo Talent Plan and is used to scout and manage riders. The six points of the Talent Guide are:

### 1  Riding Skills

Anyone can learn to ride and improve their skill with training to some degree. However, some riders are naturally more talented than others. We still do not know a lot about why this is, but we assume that these differences exist because of inherent qualities such as physical coordination, a "feel" for balance, and reaction speed. However, inherent traits or talent is not enough. Many talented riders disappear from the sport after a time. We have a saying: "Talent spoils the rider." Riders whose talent initially gave them an advantage are often surpassed later by riders who have less talent but more dedication.

## 2  Horse Knowledge

You have to know a lot about horses in order to learn how to "sense" them. A world-class rider has natural authority and quickly inspires confidence in his horse—a kind of "horse whisperer." Fortunately, if you are not born with this aptitude, much of this "skill" can be learned.

## 3  Motivation/Desire to Improve

Research on Olympic riders has shown that motivation is the most important quality for success. A person who is prepared to work day and night to improve has the best chance of doing so. Therefore, as mentioned in (1), the most talented people are not always the ones who are successful, but those who have worked the hardest.

## 4  Performing under Pressure

"He was so nice in the warm-up but fell apart as soon as we entered the ring," is a statement frequently heard at shows. Nevertheless, every performance must be observed in the arena if you want to build a successful show career. Fortunately, this skill can be improved by good mental coaching and lots of experience.

## 5  Management/Entrepreneurial Skills

We have already talked about money. Just as in motor racing, money, unfortunately, is an important part of equestrian sport. Horses are very expensive, both to buy (particularly good ones) and to maintain. For this reason, top riders are also managers and entrepreneurs. They buy and sell horses or give lessons to finance their sport (and write books, like we do). Showing horses at the Olympic level is therefore a multi-faceted profession.

## 6  Team Building/Social Skills

You cannot make it alone at the top of the horse world; it is a team sport. First, you are dependent on a good horse, for which you need either a sponsor or your own money to buy. You also need a trainer, grooms, a farrier, a vet, and perhaps other support people. If you cannot organize and fund such a team, then you do not have a chance.

## In Order to Succeed You Must G.R.O.W.

When you have set a goal, it is wise to determine all the things you need to do to achieve it. Start by going through the Talent Guide (above) and see if you can realistically achieve your goals in the sport. Learn how you fit into the hierarchy of equestrian sport by answering the following questions, which form the foundation of the GROW Model, the growth system that many modern coaches use for their students.

### Goal

- What is your long-term goal?
- When do you want to achieve it?
- Have you made a step-by-step plan?
- What does success look like in the short term?
- How much personal control do you have in achieving success?
- To what extent is your goal positive and attainable?

### Reality

- What is your current situation (who, what, where, when, and how)?
- Where are your opportunities and your challenges?
- What have you done so far and with what means?
- What has been the result of your efforts?
- What are the biggest obstacles to your progress?
- What is the essence of the problem?

### Options

- What options or means do you already have at your disposal?
- What opportunities do you have for achieving your goal?
- And if you had… (more time, money, help, skills, etc.)?
- What are the advantages and disadvantages of each opportunity?
- Which opportunity do you have the best feeling about?

### Will

- When will you take the steps to achieve your goal?
- Exactly what steps will you take and have you written them down?
- Are there still obstacles, and what can you do to eliminate them?
- What help do you need? From whom and how will you get it?
- On a scale from 1 to 10, how motivated are you to take the necessary steps?
- If your motivation is not a 10, then what can you do to increase it? Or should you perhaps take a step back?

*Students enrolled in the Academy's training weeks frequently study sports psychology, which is important for lower level riders and pleasure riders, too. Riding is a mental game between two living beings. Knowledge about the other being—the horse—is necessary, but self-knowledge is just as important.*

## Conclusion

Psychology is important in equestrian sports. Training is the process of persuading your unconscious body to do what your conscious mind wants it to do. You do not have total control over your body—it "gives" itself over only after endless training and repetition. This takes a great deal of time. For this reason, patience and persistence are important qualities for a rider. You can only be a good rider when your body and mind are in balance with one another.

Psychology also plays a major part in the relationship between rider and horse. As a rider, you need to learn how to understand your horse to the fullest extent possible. You can only tell your horse what you want from him when you can adapt to the habits of a herd animal and if you can control your body and mind—skills that require a rider to go through an intense learning process. Many riders sit on a horse without the necessary knowledge about horses, themselves, control, and riding skills.

One of the basic principles for becoming a good rider is knowing oneself well and "looking in the mirror" on a regular basis. Furthermore, you need to set clear goals and know how to improve yourself. Improvement requires a plan. If you truly want to improve, start by making that plan today. However, be sure that you adjust your plan regularly and that you continue enjoying the sport. Enjoyment should always be number one!

# Joep on Psychological Aspects of the Sport

I COMPLETED MY STUDIES in psychology about 35 years ago. When I finished the first part of my education in Amsterdam, I was especially interested in sports psychology and animal behavioral studies, enjoying lectures by Dr. Kortland at Artis, the oldest zoo in the Netherlands. Years later, I realized that these are still my two favorite subjects. The psychology of animal and man—horse and rider—are inextricably bound together in equestrian sports. An unsteady rider will create an unsteady horse. On the other hand, a steady horse can have a steadying influence on the rider. You cannot view these things as separate entities. Knowledge of rider psychology must be coupled with knowledge about the horse's nature.

As an equestrian journalist and Director of the World Cup, I have seldom mentioned—over more than 25 years—that I was a psychologist. Psychologists are rarely taken seriously. And, they used to be totally out of place in the serious horse world. I believe Anky van Grunsven is the main person responsible for the current popularity of psychology in equestrian sports. I will never forget how she thanked Peter Murphy for his psychological advice in an emotional press conference after she won her first Olympic gold medal in Sydney. Her comment in the press conference was published in the papers, and the reaction was huge. Psychology was suddenly "in."

The impetus Tineke received through her Master Coach training at the NOC*NSF has been very important for the Academy. Tineke learned how top coaches from other sports were successful with psychological training and guidance. At the Academy, we see a growing interest each week from students who want instruction from Rico Schuijers and me about the psychological aspects of riding. Mental training is also one of the most important parts of the Rabo Talent Plan, which we manage, and I am convinced that the Netherlands has already benefited a great deal from this training at the international horse shows.

Riders now fill the waiting rooms of many sports psychologists. I remember a statement made by Emiel Voest, who works with many problem horses: "There aren't many problem horses; there are more problem riders. Actually, I should leave those horses alone and instead send their riders to a sports psychologist." Perhaps Emiel is right: we pay a lot of attention to training horses but little attention to training riders.

In our classes at the Academy, it often becomes apparent how few people can actually say something about the nature and personality of their horse and how poorly they know themselves. I try to expand the insight of our guests through explanation, test sheets, and practical role-playing. Some of our most amusing role-playing requires one person to act like a horse and the other to act as the trainer/rider. This often makes us double over in laughter, but every time I hear how people find it useful to be confronted with themselves this way. That is when the "light bulb" comes on: "Huh, that's how it works?"

Actually the psychology of horse and rider is fairly simple. It is mostly about skills that you already know about from "somewhere" but that are not quite ready for you to use when you need them. Try to have them ready because you must also have courage to use them!

At the 2005 Global Dressage Form, Imke gave the audience a hilarious explanation of how she applied the principles she had learned in her mental training sessions to her riding in the Athens Olympics. She prepared her warm-up for the tests in minute detail. She decided what she wanted to do and who she wanted around her. Tineke was the only one allowed to help her during her entire warm-up. She wanted Sjef Janssen there for only the last 20 minutes to go through different parts of her test. However, she found that her father just made her nervous. So Imke approached us and calmly explained how she wanted things. Her words were difficult for me to hear, of course, but then I took a seat high in the stands amongst the crowd. Fortunately, I did not feel bad for long: Imke and Lancet really outdid themselves and gave a world-class performance!

*Imke, Sjef Janssen, and Tineke during the warm-up, just before Imke's test at the Athens Olympics. Who should and who shouldn't help you in the warm-up? How long should you warm-up? What exactly should you do? And, in what order? Imke had organized everything down to the last detail in Athens: only Tineke could help her, and she asked Sjef Janssen to come the last half-hour to fine-tune everything. Imke asked that all her other advisors be absent at that time of preparation.*

## CHAPTER 4
# Body Control: Learning to Sit

### The Independent Seat as the Foundation of Training

In the previous chapters, we tried to explain how communication works between a person and a horse. The key points outlined are: start from the horse's nature; learn to use the horse's language; and know exactly what you are doing, because for your every Action, there is a Reaction (see the Question and Answer Method on p. 77). This principle also applies to every uncontrolled action, so before you know it, you can have a horse taught the wrong way of doing things.

A rider who has yet to develop an independent seat gives his horse numerous unintentional signals. For this reason, acquiring a correct seat is the first step toward awareness training under saddle. In this chapter, we deal with both the theory and practical instruction of Australian trainer Richard Weis, which have been further developed at the Academy in cooperation with Inge Jansen-Bouwmeester of the Dutch Equestrian Federation.

### Body Balance and Tension

In one of history's oldest equestrian texts, the Greek general Xenophon wrote that the ideal seat is much more like standing with one's legs slightly bent and spread than it is like sitting on a chair. This is an important observation about a rider's position, and Richard Weis agrees: sitting on a horse has more to do with standing than sitting! The rider sits straight in the saddle so that a vertical line can be drawn through his ear, shoulder, hip, and heel. The rider sits directly above the horse's center of gravity. This requires the so-called "body balance" of the muscles, which allows a rider to sit up nice and tall, yet swing elastically with a horse's movement in the most relaxed way possible.

There is an important distinction between body balance and tension, something which is learned through lots of practice and good instruction. Body balance means that your muscle tone is so balanced that you can maintain an optimum position in the saddle without becoming tense. Correct body balance of the major core muscles is the only way to keep your hands and legs as still as possible. The more still your hands and legs are, the faster the horse can perceive your aids. Hands and legs should

*Richard Weis, a certified teacher of the Alexander Technique, points out areas of Imke's neck and head position that could be improved. He is the expert on an independent seat. Richard says that your body is the "instrument" you use to tell your horse what you want him to do. You need to practice a lot in order to be able to use that instrument really well.*

only be used in a relaxed and completely independent manner while the rest of the body acts as a shock absorber. Your upper body, hands, and lower legs stay as still as possible because they remain relaxed and independent of your core. To develop a stable seat, you mainly have to learn how to follow a horse's movement; that is, to move with your horse. This takes place primarily in the core of your body.

Use of the term "shock absorber" sometimes wrongly encourages a rider to move his hips front and back as well as to move in various other undesired ways unrelated to the movement of the horse. Richard Weis prefers to use the words "follow" or even "invite." The rider's body should move "unconsciously" with the motion of the horse's back, which requires the rider to sit as quietly as possible. The horse, not the rider, indicates the movement. Richard Weis sometimes illustrates the way the rider's seat moves with the horse by attaching white balls to the saddle where the seat bones and calves are normally located. When the moving horse is viewed from the side, it becomes apparent from the motion of the balls how the seat bones and the calves should move. This is a good demonstration. If you sit correctly in the saddle, the horse's body automatically indicates the movement. We will come back to this later.

## Self-Carriage

One goal of training is for the rider to gain more influence over the horse through seat and leg aids and rely less on the reins. Actually, both horse

*An independent seat requires balance. Most riders at the Academy have had some experience jumping horses, and they still ride regularly in a two-point seat, which facilitates a feel for balance. Tineke thinks that more dressage riders should do this. In this photo taken in the summer of 2004, she is riding Sunrise over cavaletti. The pair were showing Prix St. Georges at the time.*

*Here are Imke and Sunrise in a training session and during their test at the 2006 Dutch Dressage Championship in Eindhoven, which they won. The position of the rider's body on the horse is more like standing than sitting. The rider's feet are oriented toward the ground. If we were to magically make Sunrise disappear, Imke would land in a standing position with her feet on the ground.*

and rider must develop self-carriage so that they can maintain their balance and movement without help or support. It is a natural reaction for the rider to use the reins for support. For this reason, beginning young riders at the Spanish Riding School are taught for months on the longe line without their reins. The basic principle adhered to is to create a rider in balance, who can let his body become supple and "spring-like," maintain the same rhythm, make himself long, and still stay actively relaxed while sitting up straight (see p. 67). This lays the foundation; however, the rider must still learn to organize his body in such a way that he can give aids with his hands, legs, and weight in the most optimum way.

Leaning forward or backward hinders the correct effect of the aids on the horse, and gripping with your legs is unproductive, too. The position of the body in the sit-stand position should be oriented to the ground. It is helpful to go through the exercise of letting your body weight drop into your feet and through them to the ground. Let us imagine that your horse suddenly vanishes from underneath you. If that were to happen to you while sitting in the correct seat, you will land upright exactly on your feet. Let gravity do its work!

The only correct basis from which you can give your aids is an independent seat. In addition, the rider's body must stay in perfect balance without tension exactly above the center of gravity.

The correct position of a rider on a horse is more like standing than sitting. It is helpful to go through the exercise of letting your body weight drop into your feet. Orient yourself to the ground through your feet. Pretend that if your horse disappears from under you at any second you are ready to land on your feet without falling forward or backward. Let gravity do its work!

## Backpacks and Abdominal Muscles

Balance is the result of the "cooperation" between the muscles in the front and back of the body. In addition, the abdominal muscles hold the internal organs against their support point, which is the spine. The same principle

*The position depicted in the drawing in the middle shows the rider sitting directly above the horse's center of gravity. This is the basic position and the one that most resembles standing. In the first drawing, the rider is sitting "heavier," which puts more stress on the horse's hindquarters. This position, combined with a rein aid, should only be used as a slowing aid. The drawing on the right shows the rider in a somewhat lighter seat, which is often used to take weight off the horse's back. It is also a good way to reward a horse, along with a softer hand or a pat on the neck. The second two drawings show positions most conducive to ideal balance. The first drawing with the upper body somewhat behind the vertical tends to make the rider lose balance and grab the reins.*

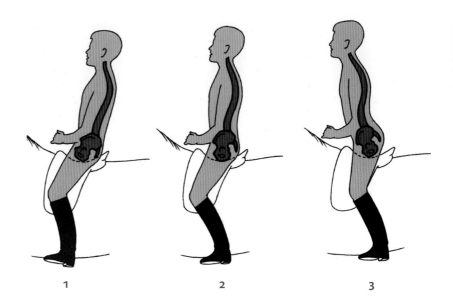

applies to horses: in collection, the abdominal muscles strengthen the connection between the front and back of the horse. Strengthening the abdominal muscles allows the hind legs to step farther under the body.

Richard Weis developed an exercise for those unfamiliar with dressage to illustrate this point: "Ask the person to do the following exercises with his knees slightly bent: first do a pirouette with one foot on the ground, like a Western horse doing a spin. Then do a pirouette, picking up each foot and putting it down again. Perform this exercise a couple of times. The person will soon feel the effort required from the leg and back muscles and realize that a horse's hindquarters must have the strength of a weightlifter in order to support that heavy body with flexed joints."

The stomach muscles of the horse as well as those of the rider must be strong. Riders must ensure that their core is stabilized, which allows their weight aids from their seat bones to flow through their legs and—just like the horse—receive the weight through bent knee and ankle joints. Their muscles from the pelvis to the chin hold the contents of the abdominal cavity in the chest "up and back," close to the spine. Richard Weis uses the words "up and back" because he believes it is very important that every rider is aware that their total body weight can only be supported through connection with the skeletal frame.

Compare the rider's body with an old-fashioned type of backpack that had a metal structure supporting the canvas. The supporting structure of the body, from which all power ultimately originates, is the spine. The abdomen, like a backpack, is filled with various loose contents. To keep these contents from getting in the way, the backpack must be attached to the spine as closely as possible. Our stomach muscles function like the canvas of a backpack. They keep the vital organs "up and back" against the spine so that they stay very near the back.

People who ride many horses each day not only have strong back muscles but also strong stomach muscles, which is something that Tineke learned thirty years ago during her studies at the Academy for Physical Education. However, we were recently faced with this fact again by coincidence. Joep has maintained an almost daily fitness program for many years, which includes cycling, jogging, and working out in his home gym. When Joep got a new piece of exercise equipment, Tineke playfully decided to find out how many sit-ups she could do: more than Joep, despite all his training!

Some riders hold their breath to compensate for lack of proper abdominal muscle support. This does not work: although the vital organs might stay tight, the rider becomes winded and must stop to rest.

## Spring Action

A short wheel base improves a car's maneuverability. This also applies to the movement of the horse. A short "wheel base" allows a horse to perform a pirouette. The horse shifts weight from his forehand onto his hindquarters. He then becomes more compact, his wheel base shorter, allowing him to turn easily. A horse can only become compact like this by contracting his abdominal muscles—his body then becomes "rounder," which means that his topline stretches. The forces that are transmitted through the skeleton become bigger.

Under such circumstances, changes occur in the horse's skeleton. The spine lengthens and functions more like a spring. The body is then "pumped up" rather than "flattened down."

The same process also occurs in the rider. When his body is stretched, there is a danger of it becoming tense and stiff, something which will certainly happen if we do not keep the example of the elastic spring in mind.

A rider's body that lengthens in the correct manner—that is, upward and downward—functions like a spring. It springs in movement upward and downward. When the horse moves forward, the rider's body takes the horse "forward and up" with him, so to speak. The rider sits up straight, exactly above the horse's center of gravity. The basic principle is that the rider's weight moves upward and downward through the back of the body. Weight travels upward through the spine, neck, and the top of the head—as though the crown of the head were being pulled to the ceiling by a rope on a pulley. The rider's downward moving weight is received

We can compare the rider's body with an old-fashioned type of backpack with a metal structure supporting the canvas. The supporting structure of the body is the spine. The abdomen, like a backpack, is filled with various loose contents. Our stomach muscles function like the canvas of the backpack.

*The rider's body needs to move up and down like a "spring" as Richard Weis demonstrates here. The rider takes the horse "forward and up" with him, so to speak. He invites the horse to move bigger through his "spring-like" action.*

The rider's body moves upward and downward in motion like a spring. When the horse moves forward, the rider's body takes the horse "forward and up" with him, so to speak. This process is interrupted if the rider's lumbar area becomes too hollow or too round. When this happens, the body "separates" into two uncoordinated parts: the part above the lumber area and the part below. As a result, the spring action is lost.

through the spine, pelvis, seatbones, feet, and stirrups.

Richard Weis says that the rider can "invite," so to speak, bigger movement from his horse through this "spring action." For example, Anky van Grunsven illustrates this concept well. Her body has good spring action; as a result, she takes her horses forward and upward. You can experience this feeling on the ground—or better yet, on a trampoline—by taking small jumps forward while maintaining correct rider position.

In the saddle, it is very important that the rider's lower back transmits weight correctly to the seat bones and stirrups. This process can be interrupted when the lower back/lumbar area becomes too hollow. A hollow back leads to the body "separating" into two uncoordinated parts: the part above the lumber area and the part below. As a result, the spring action is lost. Such is also the case when the opposite occurs, when the lumbar area moves forward and back too much. The ideal body balance allows the rider's body to remain straight without tension. The pelvis, which can tilt forward and back, is then in the "middle position," so to speak. The lumbar area should be neither hollow nor round.

## Your Body as an Instrument

The rider's back can only be strengthened by lengthening and shortening the body and the muscles. This is a complicated process, which is only possible through a long-term training program. However, few riders are able to really develop themselves and their horses. The problem is often in the rider's position, in particular, instability in his core. However, it can also lie in an inability to control the arms so that the rider can maintain quiet and independent hands in all circumstances. There are many details that can stand in the way of an optimum and effective seat.

We cannot go into all these details in this book, but it is certainly interesting to observe the physical principles that Richard Weis names concerning the rider's position and movement, as these are the cause of most riding problems. And if these riding problems are not solved, the rider cannot develop the horse. Richard Weis uses the Training Scale (see sidebar) for riders as well as horses. He says, "You'll understand a bit more what you ask from a horse if you've experienced the six points of the Training Scale with your own body. When that is the case, you'll have a better understanding of what it is to ask a horse to do dressage."

More riders should take interest in the athletic aspect of the cooperation between rider and horse. "Work on yourself and play with your horse!" Richard reveals that he "borrowed" that sentence from a Western trainer. The principle behind the concept is as follows: the only thing that is available to you when you are sitting on a horse is your body and the will that directs it. Your body is your instrument. Train your body to do what you want to accomplish with your horse. Train yourself to train your horse!

**The only thing that is available to you when you are sitting on a horse is your body and the will that directs it. Your body is your instrument. Train your body to do what you want to accomplish with your horse. Train yourself to train your horse!**

## The Training Scale for Riders

Exercises and examples usually clarify meanings much better than theoretical explanation. Nowadays, top riders do more to keep physically fit. And there are riders who do exercises to imitate the physical experience of riding.

Several years ago, top rider Sven Rothenberger prepared for his shows by doing his dressage tests himself, on the ground without a horse, including piaffe and flying changes. At first, some of his colleagues laughed at him, but later, they understood that this was excellent mental preparation. Sven did his tests on the ground to check how well he knew them, but riders can also do this exercise to practice the feeling they need in a test. Let us compare this to a practice swing in golf. In golf, the club is the instrument, and you practice without a ball. In riding, the body is the instrument, and you practice without a horse. Richard Weis goes a step further: he believes that if you want to understand the Training Scale you have to experience it yourself. You can put Richard Weis'

advice into practice by thinking up several of your own exercises. We have done this, and here are the results:

### 1 Rhythm and Regularity
Exercise: Pay attention to the noise your feet make on the ground—they should sound exactly the same and in rhythm. You can alter the rhythm at times but make sure that you maintain the same rhythm for at least 10 steps and that you keep moving in the correct position—that is, upright.

### 2 Relaxation and Suppleness
Exercise: Practice your body "feel" by alternating between tension, relaxation, and body balance. Go from a tense, stiff position to the correct rider position with a balanced body and then let your body completely relax. Let your shoulders drop and your arms hang. Alternate between relaxation and tension, and imprint the feeling you get in your memory.

### 3 Contact

Exercise: Stretch your body: make your neck long but not stiff; sit down and stand up again, walk, and sit down again; maintain the same upright position. Play a little with tension, body balance, and relaxation. Your body is in the right condition if you can achieve maximum length without tension.

### 4 Impulsion

Exercise: Elevate and lengthen your strides at a trotting speed; experiment with the exercise, alternating between a tense body and a relaxed body, but ensure that you maintain the correct position; that is, straight.

### 5 Straightness

Exercise: Try to sit exactly straight, then stand, and walk straight ahead. Ask someone to watch you, and you will see that this exercise is almost impossible. The hip or shoulder on one side is usually lower than the other.

### 6 Collection

Exercise: Imitate a kangaroo for one minute. First, hop in place using both legs together as a warm-up. Then hop up a few steps of a stairway. Start with a few steps, and you will discover that this exercise demands a great deal of concentrated vertical energy in order to complete it well. This energy goes upward through the top of your head, so to speak.

Experiment with hopping while keeping your head between your shoulders, curling your toes, or clenching your jaws together. Notice if hopping becomes more difficult and listen to the sound of your feet landing on the ground. You will become aware that small tensions can bring about big changes.

After doing this exercise for 20 minutes, you will have much greater respect for the kangaroo, and you will see the need for learning good body control in order to make your hops bigger and smaller. What you are doing is playing with your balance and, in fact, "collecting" yourself by making your hops bigger and smaller.

## In Search of Blockages

Before we give more consideration to the rider in motion, let us first take a closer look at the movement of the horse's back. We know from equine biomechanics that the horse's vertebrae move very little, and the forces exerted on its back are so great that its body is designed to hold the back as stable as possible.

A thorough understanding of equine biomechanics is not critical for riders, as long as they can learn to feel what is happening in the horse's body. Riders get this information through the movement of the spine from which they can feel any tension or blockage, and they need to learn to feel where these blockages are located and how to solve them. The spine articulates in wavelike motions, which are more symmetrical the straighter a horse is; in other words, the spine makes the exact same wave motions both left and right. When a rider is able to shorten and collect a horse, he also gets symmetry in the movement of the spine upward and downward. Rhythm and regularity are connected with symmetry.

Physical details have a major influence on the horse (see photo below), which is why we consistently teach our horses to respond to different hand positions. For example, "wide" hands as shown here are used for a lower head position. When a horse's head goes down, the rider's hand position automatically lowers too so the line from the elbow to the snaffle ring remains straight.

Shortcomings in a rider's position can lead to major riding problems when uncorrected because the trainer does not notice them. An important detail is the rider's ability to carry his shoulders, elbows, and wrists in such a way so as to maintain "independent" hands under all circumstances. Soft hands are created by the shock-absorbing qualities of the shoulder, elbow, and wrist joints.

The rider's weight aids should flow through the legs and feet. The ankles function as shock absorbers. Small details are very important: for example, when your toes are tense inside your boots their shock-absorbing action is blocked.

Richard Weis focuses a great deal of attention on the rider's neck and head position. The effect of keeping your head upright with a relaxed neck radiates throughout your entire body. Lengthening your body while maintaining a relaxed seat, increases the space between your vertebrae, and this increases the "spring action." Tineke often uses the following analogy in her teaching: "Pretend the top of your head is being pulled to the arena ceiling by a rope on a pulley."

*Imke is riding Lancet through a corner. She places her weight a little to the inside, making her inside leg become like an axis, as it were, around which the horse turns.*

Tension in the horse's body disrupts the symmetrical wavelike motions. Disruption causes crookedness. This crookedness becomes worse as we ask a horse for more collection, which often leads to rhythm mistakes or what is referred to as "rein lameness." To help resolve this issue, the rider needs to go back a step and relax the horse in order to loosen the muscles again and get rid of the blockage on whichever side of the horse's body it occurs. You have to develop a feel for this; in other words, you must learn how a straight horse feels and keep that straightness as a guiding principle in training.

## Discover the Wave Motion

The straightness we strive for with our horses concerns the entire spine, both horizontally (left to right) as well as vertically (top to bottom). The wavelike motion or the "swing" is the action necessary to coordinate the limbs. The rider is part of this swing, as it were, as he sits in the middle of the horse's body, and his legs swing with the wavelike motion of the horse.

The movement of the horse's body makes the swinging of the horse's legs possible. A hind leg can only move forward when it is not bearing any weight; therefore, the horse swings its barrel to the right when its left hind leg steps forward. At that point, the right hind leg is on the ground and in the position to bear all the weight. If we understand this principle, we can also learn how to feel it.

Every rider should automatically be able to feel which hind leg is on the ground at any moment. Try this exercise on your horse by saying "left" or "right" at the moment that the corresponding hind leg is on the ground. You will be surprised how difficult this is. The rider sits above all the subtle movements of the horse's body, so it is useful to study the timing and direction of the movements and learn how to feel them. When the horse's barrel swings to the outside, space is created under the rider's inside seatbone and inside leg, allowing the rider to sit deeper to the inside. Then, the wavelike motion swings to the other side, like a pendulum, and raises the inside of the rider's body, including the seat bone and foot. The rider's pelvis and legs swing, too, with left-side and right-side movements alternating up and down.

Stand behind a horse being ridden at the trot and you will see subtle left-right movements of the rider's hips. One seat bone and foot will be lower than the other; next, the rider's entire body will move up and then down; then the other seat bone and foot will be lower. The seat bones and calves move upward, then forward, and then down, as though they were going over a speed bump. All the joints participate in the spring action of the rider's body and are rhythmic in their entirety. The rider's body must work like a spring; otherwise, these upward-forward arcs of the seat bones and calves are not physically possible. You can see the relationship between the movements well—left-up, right-down—by standing behind a moving horse.

## Crooked Times Crooked Equals Straight

Richard Weis has an insightful saying: "Dressage is the art of putting one crooked body on top of another crooked body and making both bodies straight." He states his idea in this provocative manner to point out clearly that the rider is usually just as crooked as the horse! Often riders can easily sit deep on one seat bone but not the other. (Most usually have more difficulty with the left seat bone—and when you look higher up that side of their body, you will see most likely that tight muscles are pulling that shoulder down and the hip up.) Work on a circle illustrates uneven seat-bone weight the best: a rider's weight tends to fall to the outside on a circle; however, in order to correctly bend a horse around a circle, the rider must place more of his weight toward the inside. When the rider does not do this correctly, his inside hip "collapses."

What a rider needs to do to shift his weight to the inside when riding a curved line, is lengthen his body on the inside, receive weight from the outside, and drop that weight down into the inside stirrup. This extra weight strengthens and stabilizes his body on the inside, allowing that side to function like an "axis"—imagine a fixed line formed by the inside shoulder to the inside foot, including the inside leg. The outside of the rider and the outside of the horse turn around this axis. In Richard Weis' opinion, aids applied to the outside of the horse are only effective when they are supported by a good axis on the inside.

Richard notices that he gets better results when he stops talking about turns in his lessons and instead focuses attention on getting the horse absolutely straight, which is to say that the rider must be able to use the aids to put the horse "straight between both legs." The rider's legs should never be fixed and rigid like a wall; on the contrary, they should be relaxed and hang loosely on the horse's sides, yet ready to respond immediately with a very quick aid in the form of a touch or squeeze, when needed.

Riding a good curved line also becomes easier from this position. The correct bend is created when the front of the horse's head follows the direction of the circle, like the rider's shoulders and pelvis. The axis formed by the imaginary fixed line from the inside shoulder down to the inside foot keeps the horse from falling to the inside. When the horse can no longer fall to the inside or outside, the correct curved line is automatically created.

All this sounds rather difficult, but it boils down to the rider assuming the correct physical position for the movement desired and diligently keeping that position until the horse understands what is being asked of it. The horse is shaped within the framework of the applied aids. The rider's legs function like flexible "walls." Energy is generated from back to front and "drives" the horse's body into the path created by the rider's legs.

In instances where the hind legs do not follow the track of the front legs—and Richard is not referring to lateral movements but crookedness in the horse—moving the forehand with the reins in front of the hindquarters is far more useful than attempting the opposite, unless the horse's hindquarters are swinging out. Training is ultimately aimed at making the forehand light and maneuverable.

## Conclusion

The position of a rider on a horse has more to do with standing than sitting! In theory, the rider sits straight in the saddle so that a vertical line could be drawn through his ear, shoulder, hip, and heel. The rider sits straight above the horse's center of gravity, which requires so-called "body balancing" of the muscles. Body balance allows you to sit up nicely, yet swing elastically with a horse's movement in the most relaxed way possible.

*Imke with Sunrise at the 2006 National Championships. A vertical line can almost be drawn through Imke's ear, shoulder, hip, and heel. She is sitting quite nicely above her horse's center of gravity with her weight somewhat toward the front of the saddle. However, even more important for a functional seat is muscular body balance, which is quite evident in this photo. Body balance means that your muscles enable you to sit up as straight as possible yet swing with the horse's movement in a relaxed and elastic manner, and your body contains optimum "spring action."*

Your hands should stay quiet and next to each other at a good height, thumbs turned up, hands closed, fingers around the reins, and wrists to the outside. There should be a vertical line down from the hands, through the knees, to the toes. In the walk, trot, and canter, the hands remain still relative to the horse's mouth.

Your upper legs lie still, relaxed, and turned in, with the flat side of the thigh bone against the saddle. The knee is the stable point. The lower legs hang loosely and quietly against the horse's sides in the same line as the hands and knees. Do not pinch with your legs! The feet rest relaxed in the stirrups, supported on the ball of the foot. Keep your heels down and your toes pointed inward in a relaxed manner.

A rider's body that lengthens in the correct manner—that is, downward and upward—functions like a spring. It "springs" up and down in movement. When the horse moves forward, the rider's body takes the horse "forward and up" with him.

**In closing, here are a few characteristic Richard Weis sayings:**

- Take your horse with you like the lead dancer in the tango.
- Enjoy your horse's swinging back (love to bounce).
- Move upward with your horse and invite your horse to let his back swing.
- Let your weight sink to your feet through your spine and seat bones.
- If I were to make your horse magically disappear, you should land on your feet.
- Pay attention to the details: relax your toes in your boots.
- Your body is your instrument.
- Train your body to do what you want to do with your horse.
- Train yourself to train your horse!
- Work on yourself and play with your horse!

# Tineke on Richard Weis

RICHARD WEIS CAME TO us by way of the German trainer Johann Hinnemann. Richard gave clinics at the Horse Event and stayed several weeks at the Academy. It was a bit strange for an Australian to become so successful at putting on clinics in Germany and the Netherlands. He also thought this accomplishment was remarkable and joked about it, laughing heartily.

The lessons he gave were impressive. I was the first to feel that something unusual was happening under my saddle: our breeding stallion Broere Jazz began to move more freely after I followed Richard's instructions. At first, we had looked a bit askance at Richard when he had us jump like kangaroos through the Academy library, but then we began to follow him with more interest.

Richard is not only an experienced horseman; he also works with the Alexander Technique, which is a cross between physical therapy and kinetics. In addition, his didactic talents make him unique. He argues for more understanding of the horse, using "smaller" aids, and being less of a hindrance to the horse. Our views dovetail seamlessly in a process that started years ago.

After a long discussion at our kitchen table, we translated several passages from our previous Academy book for Richard. He reacted with surprise. We appeared to have practically the same basic principle: that is, a supple and "unforced" seat is the foundation of every horse performance. This seat is mainly about dynamic balance and not what appears to be a correct, but what is, in reality a stiff, "false" position. For example, you may have a textbook-perfect position but still be unable to effectively influence your horse. As I've mentioned, I refer to this kind of rider as "an old stick"—correct by the book but without feel.

The opposite is also possible. There are riders whose seats are not entirely "textbook," yet they can still ride well. However, in general, a correct, independent seat is still one of the most important basic principles necessary for riding well.

As a former physical education teacher, what has stayed with me is the attention Richard Weis gives to internal blockages. He looks and feels, and then determines precisely where these blocks are in your body. Tense, curled toes affect your whole body. Raised shoulders block the entire spine.

Your body is the instrument with which you tell your horse what to do. As far as that is concerned, the training of the rider is based on the exact same principle as the training of the horse.

You must determine where the blockages are and break them up through gymnastic exercises. There is still a lot of work to be done. I see an increasing number of students who are out of shape, stiff, overweight, or too tense. Of course, these conditions affect the seat. Every rider—with help from his instructor—needs to figure out what exercises (or other sports) will help solve his individual problems. For this reason, Imke swims regularly and Anky works out in the gym. A good sports massage therapist can also offer solutions. I am convinced that a rider first has to loosen and develop his own body before he can improve his horse's body.

You must have a relaxed seat before you can learn to feel your horse's wavelike motion and develop a "feel" for the blockages in his body. This is the most important principle of our training method: feel blocks and solve them. You then become your horse's fitness trainer or physical therapist of sorts. However, you will only be successful if you start with your own body!

## CHAPTER 5

# Training with the Question and Answer Method

## What Is Your Goal?

The FEI is the highest authority in equestrian sports, and the FEI rulebook details the agreements made between member nations. Article 401 of that rulebook describes the goal of dressage. It begins as follows:

*"The object of dressage is the development of the horse into a happy athlete through means of harmonious training. As a result, it makes the horse calm, supple, loose and flexible, but also confident, attentive and keen, thus achieving perfect understanding with his rider."*

To summarize, the FEI wants us to develop our horses athletically and ensure that they enjoy their work. Achieving these goals does not happen automatically. You must have a very good understanding of what exactly you want to achieve and *how* you can achieve it. You cannot simply apply human kinetics to the horse, as its body and mind are essentially different from ours. In chapter 2, we discussed the horse's specific attributes as a flight animal and herd animal, and in chapter 6, we will give more attention to the horse's anatomy. In this chapter, we will look at how horses best learn.

Fortunately, we are seeing more literature about how horses learn. It is clear that punishment and force does not make any horse happy, which is indeed one similarity shared with people. Human athletes learn and train the best when they enjoy what they do. Horses also learn best with positive training methods—that is, consistent use of a reward system.

## Make Learning Fun

Have you ever spent time at a dolphinarium? Trainers teach these big mammals all kinds of tricks by using buckets full of fish. This is a compelling example of positive learning. Can this method also be applied to training horses? If so, then how is it done?

When you incrementally give a horse treats between his front legs

*Top riders Edward Gal and Hans Peter Minderhout are having fun with dolphins. Training these mammals is very interesting and educational but different from training horses. Given that dolphins can be trained only from a distance, their trainers rely solely on positive reinforcement by rewarding them with food (a primary reward). They ignore a dolphin's mistakes and wait until it performs a workable movement. Trainers who work with horses (or elephants and camels, for that matter) use both positive and negative reinforcement. The close working proximity to these animals allows a trainer to use pressure to elicit the "Target Behavior" and as soon as the animal responds with this desired reaction, the trainer removes the pressure.*

close and then closer to the ground, you can teach him to kneel in a few weeks by steadily lowering the level at which you feed the treat. After a few weeks of practice, some horses will just kneel automatically; it is how they "beg" for a treat. When you know exactly what you want from your horse—to kneel as in this example—then you only have to know the best way to use a treat.

First, you must know exactly what you want, and if you can also make the learning process pleasant for your horse by rewarding him at precisely the right time, you are on the right training path. You are playing the fun Question and Answer game.

People often talk about horses in human terms. Some riders even talk to horses as though they were people. However, you will never understand horses if you do not learn to understand their nature. As we have discussed in previous chapters, people, as predatory animals, need to learn to understand the flight animal. Horses are limited in their ability to adapt to us, but we can certainly adapt to them. This is not easy but certainly worth the effort.

Sometimes, it appears as though horses can do clever things—or even reason—just like people. When a horse opens the latch on his stall door by using his lips and tongue, it may seem as though he figured it out on purpose. However, a horse is not capable of premeditation. This sort of reasoning is based on an ability to contemplate or analyze. Or—in the example of the latch—to store visual impressions in the brain and try to think of a solution. People are capable of doing this, as they can use the part of their brain—the prefrontal cortex—capable of this function.

When a horse undoes the latch by luck (usually as a result of idle fiddling with it for some time), then is rewarded with an opened stall door, he will pretty soon be able to open it whenever he pleases. He's figured it out because he obtained a *reward*—the door opening—from something he did himself, and this reward commits to memory the act of fiddling with the latch.

## How Does a Horse Learn?

Some horse books suggest that you ride as follows: "Slide your right leg back, squeeze with your left leg at the girth and your horse will pick up the canter." In practice, however, riders do not always understand why the horse canters when they do this. In fact, he might not. Many horses don't come with "automatic buttons" to press, and they could, just as easily have learned to canter from a whispered "canter" in their ear, or by having their ear pinched. It all depends what they were taught.

For this reason, it is especially interesting to find out how the learning process works and how you can "install a button" to make your horse canter. You can choose to make him canter from your leg, voice, or from a completely different aid. It is helpful to know and understand different teaching systems. Riders use them all, but should evaluate why, how, and when.

1 Habituation
2 Classical Conditioning
3 Operant Conditioning

### 1 Habituation: Getting Used to Girth Pressure

*Habituation* is the simplest form of training. It is the process by which a horse becomes accustomed to a stimulus, or learns to ignore a natural reaction to a stimulus. For example, horses instinctively react to a tightening girth by expanding their barrel against its pressure or even by bucking. However, a horse does ultimately get used to a girth because it remains in place and its pressure does not increase. Looking at it another way, the same principle applies to cavaletti poles stacked in the corner of an arena. The horse sees the poles and spooks at them the first few times, but when the poles do not get "worse" and do not "attack" him, he gets used to them being there. This is the way that police horses get used to noise, umbrellas, smoke, and other such potentially threatening items. It is, of course, a useful form of training.

### 2 Classical Conditioning: The Rider Takes the Initiative

*Classical Conditioning* combines a stimulus with an animal's reaction. Take, for example, the case of Pavlov's dogs: a bell was rung just before food was offered and the dogs salivated when they saw the food. After a few more times, the dogs also started to salivate just from the sound of the bell—no food in sight. This type of reaction is called *association* and occurs when stimuli are combined as in this case with two items: the bell and food. In Classical Conditioning, association is used by the trainer taking the initiative and creating the association. "Clicker training" is a form of this and is used quite often in the training of dogs. The clicker (a small handheld device that makes a clicking sound) functions like the bell and initially it is clicked when the dog is given a treat. After a while, the dog associates the click with the food, and the clicker itself becomes the reward, or at least, it becomes the signal of a *delayed* reward as the clicker method needs to be "reconfirmed" regularly with food.

When riding, take the example of the way the whip is used. You can encourage the horse to react by going forward—from a whip in your hand (or in an assistant's on the ground), and then "transferring" this reaction to your leg aids alone by first combining whip and leg, and then letting the whip slowly fade away. Here's another example, this time while longeing. When you say "whoa" to your horse, at the same time you "make" him stop by aiming him into a corner of the fence. You can, in the same way, transfer the reaction from the corner doing the "stopping" to your voice by diminishing the influence of the corner. After a while, your horse will stop just from your voice. This process is also called

*"Habit formation" is the simplest form of training. It teaches a horse to become accustomed to a stimulus (as Imke is demonstrating in this photo). She is tightening the girth one hole. The horse gets used to more girth pressure hole by hole. He figures out that there is no sense in resisting the pressure and soon accepts the girth.*

*association.* Riders and trainers often use it, and of course we use it as well, as we do Habituation. The problem, however, with this method is that the horse frequently makes "associations" without your knowledge and often without you *wanting* him to do so. Another disadvantage is the lack of

*The best method for teaching a horse is called "operant conditioning," which means "conditioning by discovery." You could also call this method "learning by trial and error." In these photos, Imke is teaching Sunrise to piaffe. She started this when Sunrise was sufficiently developed and "open." She sends Sunrise forward and then "receives" her; as a result, Sunrise trots with shorter but more energetic strides. Sunrise does not yet fully understand how she should respond to Imke's aids, and this creates some mental and physical pressure. Instead of trotting with the short, energetic strides, she is resistant to the hand. Imke does not punish Sunrise but contains her (with neutral legs) and quietly waits for a "workable" reaction. When that reaction comes ("giving" to the hand and continuing to move), Imke immediately relaxes her hand. Imke must keep two things in mind at such an*

*important moment: never punish Sunrise for her reactions as she does not yet fully understand what Imke wants from her; and prevent Sunrise from becoming afraid. Tension should never reach the boiling point. The entire training process should maintain a playful character. Nevertheless, tension in the form of pressure has a useful function: it is a "negative reinforcement," and a horse wants to do whatever removes the tension. As soon as Sunrise takes a "workable" stride, Imke rewards her immediately by removing the pressure: she relaxes her hand, keeps her legs in neutral position, and lightens her seat a bit. This reward is called "positive reinforcement." Developing that first workable stride further through positive reinforcement and a great deal of patience ultimately leads to a workable piaffe.*

self-initiative for the horse. In our opinion, it is better to challenge the horse so he can find out by himself what reaction he should give to your aid, and then to reward him for getting it right. This system is called Operant Conditioning and it is discussed next. We believe that this method includes more freedom of choice for the horse, that is, learning by trial and error.

### 3 Operant Conditioning: The Horse Is Encouraged to Teach Himself

Operant Conditioning is a training system that "challenges" the horse by using pressure (a correction) or "encourages" by using reward. The animal thinks for himself and tries one or several "answers" or solutions in order to get rid of the pressure or obtain the reward. When a horse, on his own initiative, does something that results in him getting rid of pressure, and/ or obtaining food as a reward for doing something right, he will readily repeat that action because of the combination of *initiative and reward*. He learns by trial and error. Consider the example of the horse that learned himself to undo the latch on the stall door after trying for days or even months. He will probably never forget how to open his stall.

In our opinion, Operant Conditioning or "learning by trial and error" is the most important process when training animals. Horses have very good memories. Operant Conditioning provides excellent opportunities for horses to do their own problem solving. Here is an example: you give the horse a signal (or leg aid), challenge him, if needed, with a bit more pressure from your leg (maybe the word "pressure" signifies a bit much; just touch him with your calf again, or give "double leg aid"), and as soon as he responds with the right answer, give him a reward, which in this case, is removal of the pressure. Eventually, the "pressure" part won't be necessary. Your horse will just respond immediately to the signal because he knows or anticipates he will receive a reward, as soon as you give your aid. He learned and remembers all this because it ultimately benefited him.

As riders, we must be familiar with the different ways horses learn: Habituation, Classical Conditioning, and Operant Conditioning. A horse can only learn when the training the rider provides is clear and consistent. Operant Conditioning, especially, requires clarity and consistency.

*According to the rules of the international equestrian sports organization, the FEI, "the object of dressage is the development of the horse into a happy athlete through means of harmonious training." The Academy believes that a varied program—for example, training on a galloping track and going on trail rides—is part of achieving this goal. According to "learning theory," training is most effective when the animal (and the person) enjoys it.*

"Question" and "answer" are
the words that we think best
describe the communication
between rider and horse.
Training with four steps:
Action, Pressure, Reaction,
and Reward works so well
because you motivate your
horse positively through
reward. The horse does what
you want, not because he is
forced, but because he is rewarded. Removing pressure
is the reward, for example by
relaxing rein pressure or removing a leg aid.

Riders should know the different teaching systems: Habituation, Classical Conditioning, and Operant Conditioning. We use all systems, and we are trying to use them more consciously. In general, we prefer Operant Conditioning, which works so well because you let your horse teach himself from using his own initiative to figure out the solution. And it is immediately followed by the reward.

## Training with the Question and Answer Method (Operant Conditioning)

Emiel Voest uses the concepts of pressure and reward in his freestyle groundwork method, and through Richard Weis, we learned about publications on this subject by ethologist, equine researcher, and former top rider Andrew McLean of the Australian Equine Behaviour Centre. McLean has done a great deal of research on Operant Conditioning. His studies have shown that horses find this method an enjoyable way to learn. It encourages refinement of the aids. McLean uses the concepts *signal, pressure,* and *reward* in his system.

Training with Operant Conditioning is also a method that novice riders can apply easily, for example, Machteld van Dierendonck of the Faculty of Veterinary Medicine in Utrecht also uses this system both in treating horses with behavior problems and in her teaching. Machteld and Andrew know each other well and consult regularly on the way in which horses learn.

Training by "challenging" a horse with pressure and rewarding him for the desired response is one of the most important methods available to us. To best understand the basis of it, take the example of "going forward from the leg." It's not the pressure of the leg, but the reward in the form of removing the pressure after the horse goes forward that teaches the horse the right response. The horse does not go forward to do you a favor but to do himself a favor by getting rid of the leg pressure.

The same principle applies to the reins. The rider exerts pressure on the horse's mouth from the rein, and in order to get rid of that pressure, a horse will search for various solutions. As soon as he "gives" a little to the bit, the rider rewards him by softening his hand and removing the pressure.

Other books and articles about Operant Conditioning call this system the "stimulus-response method." We prefer to describe it as a Question and Answer game. Our training method is primarily based on the following four steps:

1 **Action**
2 **Pressure**
3 **Reaction**
4 **Reward**

Training with this system leads to a fun "game" where the Pressure part (2) becomes almost unnecessary over time and your Action (1) becomes more and more light and refined. "Question" and "answer" are the words that we think best describe the communication between rider and horse.

## Primary and Secondary Rewards

Reward is the key concept in this system; therefore, it is important to take a close look at rewards. You can best reward a horse by appealing to his primal needs of food and safety. This last—safety—is not so easy to meet, however, you can certainly supply food. Feeding a horse a treat is a *primary reward*, and all good animal trainers use food.

Immediately, when your horse does what you ask, give him a treat. If you do this well, you can teach a horse to react correctly after just a few repetitions. When it is difficult to give a treat from the saddle, you can scratch your horse's crest—also a form of primary reward as this, of course, is how horses in their natural state reassure one another and express friendship with a buddy.

You can also reward your horse with a *secondary reward* like giving a pat on the neck or saying "good." When you regularly combine this secondary reward with the primary reward, eventually they will command the same value. This process is called *association*.

As mentioned above, undoubtedly the two most natural primary rewards are *food* and *scratching the withers*. Research has shown that eating lowers a horse's heart rate and reduces stress. The *removal of pressure* is

Feeding a horse a treat is a *primary reward*. All good animal trainers use this method. As soon as your horse does what you ask, immediately give a treat. However, you can also reward your horse by scratching his crest or removing pressure from your hand or leg, for example.

*Ensure that your horse makes a connection between your question (the Action) and what you expect as the answer (the Reaction). The most important basic rules relative to this principle are: a touch of the legs means go forward, and pressure on the reins means slow down.*

*Actually, our training focuses mainly on refining this game of Question and Answer. If your horse does not give you the Reaction quickly and strongly enough, repeat your aid (Pressure) and make your horse sharper. The forward aid, in particular, needs to be sharpened repeatedly by giving your horse a very clear leg aid and allowing him to canter off nicely forward on occasion.*

very nearly a primary reward, too. Just having a person on his back can cause a horse a lot of mental pressure—when a large animal jumps on a horse in the wild, it usually means the end of his life. So for horses, pressure has terrifying significance. Consequently, you should only apply pressure in a very measured way. When pressure becomes too great and promotes tension, any schooling session is over because a tense horse can no longer learn anything.

Removal of pressure, which, for a herd animal is being able or allowed to rest, means it is safe. We believe that you can make a horse feel safe just by relaxing your hand or stopping your leg aid. A rider like Anky van Grunsven is a master at relaxing her hand and removing her leg aids with lightning-quick speed as soon as her horse gives her a workable response. When your horse does what you want, sit quietly so that he is as comfortable as possible and let him continue on his own. *One of the most common mistakes we see is when a rider continues to maintain pressure even after the horse has responded correctly and is doing what you ask of him.*


## Rewarding Refines Your Aids

Training your horse by rewarding him when he responds correctly to your question is a simple technique. The goal is to be able to *refine* your Action (use softer aids) and reduce Pressure.

If your horse does not yet know an aid, just repeat it more strongly. This puts pressure on him, and he will try to get rid of it by responding correctly. As soon as your horse finds the right answer and you reward him by *immediately* removing the pressure, you will find that next time the aid can be less strong. Ultimately pressure will no longer be necessary, and only light, subtle direction to explain what you want will be necessary.

Reward *refines*, punishment *dulls*. Given the important role that reward plays in this system, you are almost certain to get an automatic response to increasingly smaller aids. Be aware of exactly what you want to achieve and reward your horse for each small improvement. As a result, you will be able to refine entire movements.

There are still more advantages. Researchers such as Andrew McLean and Machteld van Dierendonck have discovered that this training method also works well with neurotic, frightened horses. Horses in the wild often become anxious when given inconsistent signs by their leader: as mentioned, such horses must learn to react with lightning-fast speed to the smallest signals. By cooperating with the rest of the herd a horse usually stays safe and invokes trust in the leader. So, clear and consistent signs from you, the leader, are vital in order for a horse to remain calm.

When you apply the Question and Answer method in a systematic training program, and are efficient and consistent, you will get a horse that feels safe with you. Furthermore, you will need less energy to ride, as riding becomes more comfortable.

This method of training is the best way to achieve a long-lasting "answer" to your "question." The horse's *reaction* will be solid and less vulnerable to various outside influences. This desired response occurs because you allow your horse to figure out—*on his own*—how to answer your requested *action*.

You may wonder why you cannot teach horses to react directly to an action created by your voice or body language. This is because neither of these ways of asking for an action requires you to use pressure. For example, you do not use pressure to teach your horse to stop on the longe by saying "Whoa." However, you do exert pressure with the longe line (albeit very light), or when you use the side or corner of the arena to make your horse stop. Or, when you communicate with body language by taking a step closer to the horse or by standing more in front of him (more pressure), or by moving away (less pressure). It would be so convenient if you could always use pressure this way with your body—that is, *consciously*; but, unfortunately, without knowing it, you are probably using several "*unconscious*" signals that the horse sees and "responds to," which of course cannot be repeated when you are unaware of what you have done.

*Anky is phenomenal in her understanding of "Target Behavior" and her sense of timing. She breaks down every exercise into small steps and always comes up with new elements to add to them so that no exercise ever becomes routine for her horses. Her timing with regard to teaching Target Behavior is perfect: she knows the exact moment to relax (the Reward) due to her natural insight (unconscious-competence) and excellent reaction speed (fine motor skills).*

*Timing is very important. Reward your horse as soon as possible after he shows you the desired Target Behavior, preferably within a fraction of a second. Reward your horse by softening your hand and then immediately riding on. Sometimes, however, it is good to extend the reward. When your horse does something really well, you can rest him with a bit of free walk. Doing this regularly also varies your training.*

## The "Shaping" Training System Is Like a Box of Building Blocks

The training of animals is founded on the fact that behavior is developed with a single Action (i.e. cue or signal). It is to this Action that a Reaction is trained. When the first *action* and *reaction* become confirmed, you can add another.

Question and Answer (Action and Reaction) training is like a box of building blocks. You train the reactions part by part by adding a small piece each time. This is called *shaping*. (For further and complete explanations of: Action, Reaction, Pressure, and Reward see p. 88.) You would ride a lateral movement approximately as follows:

- Ask for a forward reaction (action: one two-legs aid).
  - If needed, exert pressure (one stronger aid) with lack of or incorrect reaction.
  - Reward when reaction is good (horse goes forward) and remove the action or pressure.
- Check if the horse is soft on both reins (action: "resisting" rein aid).
  - If needed, exert pressure.
  - Reward when reaction is good (horse's mouth relaxes) by removing the action or pressure.
- Ask for positioning (action: direct rein aid).
  - If needed, exert pressure when no reaction.
  - Reward when reaction is good (horse is positioned) and remove the action or pressure.
- Check if positioning is being held by horse (action: give rein).
  - If needed, exert pressure when reaction incorrect.
  - Reward when reaction is good by removing the action or pressure.

*Target Behavior is a subject worth studying. Every exercise consists of many interim steps, which you must teach your horse in sequence and which you must repeatedly test and refine. Preparing for a half-pass requires at a minimum the following interim steps before you can actually do it with the correct positioning and bend: first, your horse must go forward from both legs; if tempo control is in order, test for suppleness on both reins; then, you can ask for positioning and teach him to maintain that positioning on his own; at that point, you can address the reaction to your lateral leg aid. Developing the half-pass further can easily take several years.*

- Ask for lateral movement (action: apply leg aid behind the girth).
  - If needed, exert pressure when reaction incorrect.
  - Reward when reaction is good (horse moves sideways) and remove the action or pressure.
- Check for horse maintaining lateral movement on his own.
  - If needed, exert pressure when no reaction (redo step above).
  - Reward for correct reaction and remove the pressure.

Teach your horse these reactions one by one, and take your time doing so. At first, you may have to ride the whole of the long side or further before you get a good reliable reaction to the first part of the lateral movement (going forward). Even going forward consists of several parts, which you develop further until your horse maintains the tempo on his own (we then say that he is "thinking" forward).

Later, you make the whole lateral exercise into one fluid movement. When you have advanced to the point that your horse starts moving

**Question and Answer training is like a box of building blocks. You train part by part by adding a small piece each time. This is called *shaping*. After every successful exercise, you reward your horse by softening your hand, removing your aids, praising with your voice, scratching his crest, or letting him walk a bit on a loose rein.**

sideways exactly at the letter, you have succeeded in getting him to react well to the first parts of the exercise (forward and positioning) *before* he reached the letter. This is important in a dressage test where this preparation determines whether or not a movement is performed well.

By following the same order of parts every time and applying aids in the same consistent manner, you are being completely clear about what you want. This means that you must be 100 percent aware of (and have control over) your aids, body motion, and body language. Only then, when you have your *actions* fully under control, can you count on efficient *reactions* from your horse. This is how you achieve an effective Question and Answer training session.

## "Waiting" Exercises

Horses trained with our method may begin anticipating parts of the exercises they have practiced—and initiate a move without being asked. You could look at it and say that your horse is "begging" for his reward, so to speak, by moving on with doing the exercise before you've given the aid. But you must remember, that as a herd animal (and consequently a team player), a horse gladly goes along with whatever their higher ranking buddy asks of them so he takes the initiative. When he starts to do this, you must teach him that he should perform an exercise *only* at your direction. You must teach him to wait.

You do this by having him continue with the previous part of the exercise the moment he tries to take the initiative. Let's say, you are doing the exercise where you canter across the centerline and halt. When your horse tries to initiate this transition to halt on his own, ride him forward instead and do the transition to halt only when he is totally forward again and is no longer expecting the aid for the halt.

Surprising your horse with a question will make him pay more attention to you. It also varies the training program, and keeps him fresh mentally. Be sure that you only reward your horse when he performs an exercise *exactly* when you ask him. This means paying close attention and being very consistent.

## The Basic Principles of Training with the Question and Answer Method

Now, we will take a closer look and review the basic principles of our training system. Question and Answer training consists of four steps:

### 1  Action ("Please Do It")

Action means "Please do it!" Know exactly what part of the exercise you want to train (known as the "Target Behavior") and then give a clear aid

Use these "waiting" exercises when you need to teach your horse to refrain from anticipating your aids. As soon as your horse tries to take the initiative, and move on to a different "part" of an exercise, immediately ask him to carry on with the previous part he was doing, and make him wait for your aid. Surprising your horse like this will make him pay more attention to you. This way, training stays varied.

Melvin had previously been shown successfully by another rider before Imke got him. However, despite his previous showing success, Imke wanted to train him differently than he had been in the past. As is evident in the photo, the muscles on the top of Melvin's neck were not very well developed and he traveled somewhat on the forehand. Furthermore, his hindquarters were not strong. He easily hollowed his back and then would get rather heavy in the hand and run right through it. As a result, tempo control was not good. Imke used the principals of Operant Conditioning: Action, Pressure, Reaction, and Reward to change Melvin. At first, she had to work with a lot of pressure, acting as negative reinforcement until she got the right reaction from Melvin, which was his moving in the new position. As soon as Melvin showed this desired Target Behavior, Imke softened her hand. This is a very long process, as it requires the development of completely different muscle groups.

This is what Imke wants: Melvin is walking long and low. She wants to prevent Melvin from raising his head and hindquarters, and she wants to build new muscles. For this purpose, she makes her hand strong when Melvin moves with his head up (Pressure) and softens her hand as soon as he drops his head (Reward). This is a long, step-by-step process and takes several years. Melvin's low position first must be confirmed; he has to learn to feel comfortable in it. Asking for difficult exercises too soon while in this position may frighten him. He first has to feel completely safe going "long and low." After quite some time, Imke begins shortening and lengthening Melvin's body to develop his muscles differently.

Here you can see the muscles near the top of Melvin's neck working when Imke shortens his neck. She must shorten and lengthen the muscles in order to develop them. There is no other way. Imke makes sure that she asks a little more each time, but for now, she does not put more pressure on Melvin than he's already accustomed to. Imke sticks with her long-term goal: lightness. However, as long as Melvin's muscling is not developed in the correct way and he has not learned how to move in the correct uphill balance without support from the reins (tested by her "giving" the hand forward), she cannot achieve optimum lightness.

*Here Imke rewards Melvin by removing pressure. When a horse demonstrates the desired Target Behavior, you should respond immediately by relaxing your hand and leg. The reward does not always have to be as big as Imke shows here, but it is wise to occasionally offer your horse a bigger one when he does something very well. So, give your horse a long rein, a pat on the neck, or a touch on the crest, and say "good." To top off the reward, you can even let him rest by walking on a long rein for a bit. Applying rewards in a timely and consistent manner automatically results in a horse that wants to work for you.*

(known as the Action*)* that is specifically intended to get the desired response (known as the Reaction). An aid, for example, is a touch with both legs. This aid asks the horse to go forward. In addition to the word "aid," you'll find that we (like many equestrian texts) have used the words "signal," "cue," or "stimulus" to mean the same thing. As already mentioned, the Question and Answer training method is sometimes referred to as the "Stimulus-Response method.*"*

### 2  Pressure ("Do It Now!")

You need to "challenge" your horse further only when he does not answer your aid; you do this by putting *pressure* on him with the same aid applied more strongly. When the first touch of your leg is not enough to get the *reaction*, repeat the aid by applying a sharper leg or even tapping him with the whip. The horse will not like this, as it causes him irritation—mental and physical pressure. Maintain this level of pressure in a calm manner until you get the reaction you desire. Do not proceed further in any exercise part until you get the correct reaction to the previous part.

An *unanswered action* must always be followed by an increase in pressure. Reward your horse only when you get a "workable" reaction (see Reaction, below). But remember that pressure should never be so strong as to cause the horse to be afraid of you!

### 3  Reaction (Response)

A correct *reaction* is when the horse responds the way in which you intended with your *action,* that is, he performed the Target Behavior. Make sure that your question is realistic and that you *immediately* reward a "workable" reaction. For example, if you ask a young horse to trot more forward but he canters off instead, that can be considered a "workable" reaction: perhaps the horse could not make the distinction between trot and canter, but at least he responded to your request to go forward.

## 4 Reward ("Thank You!")

*Reward* your horse as soon as you receive the workable *reaction* by immediately removing the *pressure*: relaxing, giving with the reins, or ceasing a driving aid.

## Training with the Question and Answer Method in Practice

To clarify this system, we will use a walk-trot transition as an example. Our goal is to trot, nothing more and nothing less. To make things as simple as possible for the horse, we'll concentrate on a single aid: a touch with both calves. This is Step 1: Action.

If the horse does not react correctly or at all to the aid, give a stronger touch with both calves, and this may be followed by a touch of the whip. This is Step 2: Pressure.

Apply pressure until the horse reacts by going forward. This is Step 3: Reaction. Be satisfied easily; be positive in the beginning even about a

To sum up: Question and Answer training consists of four steps: Step 1 is Action (the aid). Step 2—if needed—is Pressure (the same aid, but stronger). Step 3 is Reaction ("workable" answer). Step 4 is Reward (removal of pressure immediately upon receiving the Reaction).

*The Dutch Championship in Eindhoven was the first show we saw Melvin do an entire test in his "new balance." His hindquarters are more connected; he now moves uphill. His muscling also looks better, although we still would like to see more muscle development in his topline. Correct muscling is proof of correct training. Unfortunately, judges do not always evaluate muscling this way. We have seen high-scoring international horses with little muscling in the right places, namely in the upper neck and hindquarters.*

small forward response, and do not pressure the horse for too long. In any case, be very careful you do not frighten him or you will lose his trust!

Remove all pressure immediately when the horse goes forward: soften your hand and relax your leg. This is Step 4: Reward.

The biggest mistake you can make is to hang onto the reins when the horse goes forward a bit too strongly. You asked him to go forward, so when he does—even too much—you *must* reward him! When his reaction is cantering instead of trotting, for example—accept that reaction nonetheless.

Another common mistake is to keep pressure on the horse by driving him on even after he has picked up the trot, When you do this, you are applying pressure without a reward following. A horse does not learn from this. We call this a "zero aid," that is, an aid with no effect. For this reason, our trainers at the Academy sometimes say to their students during their lessons: "Take your leg off!" Removing the aid rewards the horse; furthermore, it teaches him to keep moving forward without the rider having to constantly drive him on.

## How Much Pressure Should You Use?

Although applying pressure (Step 2) should ultimately become unnecessary in this system, no rider escapes the need to apply pressure on occasion. Horses react differently to it, as they vary greatly in their sensitivity. A sensitive horse may jumps sideways when a fly touches him, while a "thick-skinned" one barely reacts to a smack of the whip.

Horses also vary in the way they react to stronger aids aimed at putting pressure on them. How do you know how much pressure to use on a given horse to get the optimum response? As previously emphasized, the most important principle to remember is to avoid frightening the horse. Therefore, start with the smallest aid possible, and add pressure incrementally. If the horse becomes frightened, you have exceeded his limit. The degree of pressure you can apply to your horse can be "read" from his reaction.

In chapter 2, we focused a great deal on Emiel Voest's theory and the four survival techniques: Flight, Fight, Freeze, and Faint. The *flight* response is the only one of these that you can occasionally permit, as long as you can settle your horse and restore his confidence within a few seconds without having to resort to rough aids. You should always avoid the *fight* response. A horse is always stronger than his rider and will therefore win the fight. *Freezing* is usually the result of major trauma. Horses that exhibit the freezing response are often the victims of inexperienced riders and should be trained only by experienced professionals. The "road back" from *freezing* to *fleeing* is by way of *fighting*, an unpleasant and dangerous business that an amateur rider should not pursue.

**Most training mistakes are made by applying too much pressure, certainly when it degenerates into roughness or violence. Every time pressure that is the result of anger or venting one's emotions is applied we decrease the chance that the horse will respond in the desired way the next time. If your horse fights or freezes, you have gone too far!**

## The Six Basic Rules of Training with the Question and Answer Method

The basic training principles we use at the Academy are similar to those of Australian scientist and trainer Andrew McLean. He has formulated the following Six Basic Rules, which we'll discuss below, step by step:

1 Action and Reaction
2 Determine Target Behavior
3 Timing
4 Consistency
5 Exclusivity
6 Proportion

### Rule 1:  Action and Reaction

Make sure the horse establishes a connection between the *action*—the aid—and the desired answer: the *reaction*. The time needed to "anchor" an action and reaction in a horse's memory varies with each horse; however, the goal is to get the horse to give you the correct reaction (the Target Behavior) by using an increasingly smaller action. In theory, this should be quite easy because horses have good memories.

It is wise to make your aids as simple as possible. A common mistake is made when we apply more than one aid at the same time (leg *and* hand, for example). This just confuses the horse and if you are not careful, his reaction may become slower or he may start "anticipating," which, as we discussed at length earlier, means the horse performs the exercise on his

*Once again, a photo of the ultimate reward a rider can give a horse. Sunrise lowers her head, and Imke immediately removes the pressure (hand soft, leg neutral) and lightens her seat a bit. This reward must be applied consistently. A horse likes a soft hand, a neutral leg, and a light seat. These teaching principles are based on the theory that a horse only does something if it benefits him. When the rider ensures that this is the case, the horse will gladly want to return to the desired position, and that is exactly our aim. This is the basic reward, which we always return to in the course of our training.*

**Teach your horse to establish a connection between one Action (aid) and one Reaction (response by doing the Target Behavior).**

own initiative, instead of waiting for your aid.

It is important that we, as riders, are in clear agreement about which aids we use. It is unwise to train a horse with personal gimmicks. In the end, every horse should be able to be ridden by different riders. We consider it a big compliment when other riders can also ride our horses well.

### Rule 2:  *Determine Target Behavior*

When you want to ride a new exercise, you must clearly work out ahead of time the steps that comprise the exercise and the aids (*actions*) you need to apply. Then, you need to think about exactly what you want to achieve or "feel" from the horse's *reaction*, and whether the Target Behavior is "acceptable."

Rule 1 must be confirmed before you can begin training Rule 2. And, all the various interim steps that comprise a complete exercise must be trained as separate Target Behaviors. You *must* take these interim steps to confirm each point, because this is where things often go wrong. Many riders want to proceed too quickly, or they try to "force" an exercise instead of giving the horse time to figure it out.

When things go wrong, you must analyze exactly where the mistake lies. Which aid elicited the incorrect response? Are you sure you worked out beforehand, and gave, the correct aids for the Target Behaviors that make up all the steps comprising an exercise?

### Rule 3:  *Timing*

Let's say you ask your horse to yield to your leg. Beforehand, you have determined the reaction you'll accept or not (see Rule 2). If he does not yield sufficiently, then correct him immediately by applying *pressure*. The correction must be well-timed—in other words, at the moment of the mistake—or at least within one second of it.

When you encourage your horse with greater calf pressure, and he reacts to it, then he must also be rewarded within one second. If you wait longer to give the reward, your horse will no longer connect your aid with his yielding laterally.

A correction in the form of more calf pressure or a touch of the spur makes no sense if it is not done within one second of the horse's initial *incorrect* response. Most riders wait too long. In such cases, the horse connects the correction with another movement and therefore learns an undesired "Action-Reaction."

### Rule 4:  *Consistency*

Research shows that horses are confused by unclear instructions. As herd animals, they like a clear leader; therefore, they also like riders who train with clarity and consistency. Every time you give an aid, your horse must react in the same manner.

Do not accept a "lesser" reaction because the weather is not nice or be-

**Each aid you give must elicit the Target Behavior you need to complete a step. You need to determine ahead of time the steps that make up an exercise, and also what level of "reaction" you will find acceptable.**

**Every reward or correction must be well-timed—in other words, at the moment of the mistake—or *no later than* one second after it.**

cause you are not totally fit. The next training session, you may be feeling in top shape again and ask for a "bigger" reaction. Your horse cannot deal with this type of inconsistency because he has no way of understanding the situation—he just wants to know what he is supposed to do. If horses could talk, they might say something like: "If you would always give the aid this way, I will always react the same way, and you'll be satisfied and reward me."

Even though you may think that you are being very strict, rules and limits give a horse a benchmark. This reduces stress from uncertainty, and certainly helps him learn more easily. We are not being unkind, just simply being very clear.

*Rule 5: Exclusivity*

For every aid, there should be just one response. Reserve just one aid for one specific exercise. It is difficult for a horse to discern among a set of aids. He usually picks one out of a set and makes the connection between the aid and what he is supposed to do.

Take, for example, the transition to canter: according to traditional instructional manuals, we have to do something with our inside leg, our outside leg, our weight, and our hands. We do not think it works this way. The horse likely recognizes just one aid (for instance, the outside leg behind the girth) as *the* aid. The rest are minor details to him. Therefore, the simpler you make things, the easier your horse can learn the aid.

A horse becomes confused when the rider expects him to perform different Target Behaviors from almost the same aid. Then misunderstandings arise, such as when a horse canters instead of doing a half-pass. This happens because the aid for both exercises is the same.

Perhaps this is also the reason why so few horses "give" to the bit and have "tempo control." These two Target Behaviors need to be trained individually. (We will come back to this later on p. 106.)

*Rule 6: Proportion*

A "small" aid should be answered with a small response. And, a stronger aid should be followed by a bigger response. This reaction can always be "refined" later. Apply your aids precisely in relation to the desired effect on the horse, but always try to make them as small and invisible as possible.

A "measured" application of aids is quite undervalued in competitive dressage. Judges do not always know enough about the communication between rider and horse to judge this aspect of horsemanship well.

A rider whose aids are invisible seldom gets a better score in the Collective Marks than a rider who does not possess this skill. In practice, the horse is usually taken as the starting point from which judges score the rider. This kind of judging perhaps belongs in breed classes, where the *horse* is evaluated but *not* in the dressage ring. The dressage ring should be about the quality of communication between rider and horse!

As herd animals, horses like clear leaders; therefore, they also like riders who train with clarity and consistency.

For every aid, there should be just one response. Reserve just one aid for one specific exercise. It is confusing for the horse if the rider expects him to react one way to an assortment or various combinations of aids.

A "small" aid should be followed by a small response, and a big aid should be followed by a big response. Apply your aids precisely in relation to the desired effect on the horse, but always try to make them as small and invisible as possible.

*Imke is riding her young breeding stallion Aachen (sire: Arpeggio x Coriograf, owners: Stal Bartels, Coomans, Maree). You should immediately apply the Six Basic Rules, even with young horses (see p. 93). When you know exactly what you want, act clearly and consistently, and teach your horse to establish a direct connection between your Action and his Reaction, then you can prevent most problems.*

## The Six Basic Rules in Practice

Even when you understand the basic rules well, you cannot apply them automatically. There are many factors involved. You may be able to practice the principles of Question and Answer training in groundwork quite well; however, training from the saddle involves other aspects. Not all riders have 100-percent-control over their body. Correct application of these basic rules under saddle requires an *independent seat*—at the very least. Some riders think they have a good seat and can apply the aids they want to give; however, the reality is often something quite different.

Many riders do not realize they have a seat that is tense, crooked, stiff, or hunched over; nor do they know they inadvertently are giving aids. Seven out of 10 riders have "busy" lower legs. As long as you do not have control over your whole body, you cannot have full control over your horse. In that respect, the horse is a reflection of the rider.

Therefore, it is no coincidence that certain riders encounter the same kinds of problems when riding different horses. We know people whose horses are always "spooky," and some continually have problems with horses that rear. There are even riders who are able to develop the muscles on one side of a horse's hindquarters more than on the other side. These riders are so used to riding a crookedly developed horse that they unconsciously strive for the same feeling when on other horses.

We always compare this crookedness with the feel of riding a bicycle with a crooked pedal. When you ride one long enough, you will get so used to it that a good, new bicycle will actually feel strange. When you are crooked like this, you must first correct your seat and feel before you can correctly train a horse. The importance of a well-trained schoolmaster that allows you to know and feel exactly when you give good aids, then becomes clear.

Applying the Six Basic Rules well requires lots of practice. Riding is a sport that demands a great deal of training, and if you are on the right path, you will see it in your horse's development. In the end, the quality of the rider is always reflected by the quality of the horse. The horse mirrors the rider; when the rider does well, the horse also does well. When the horse does not perform correctly, it is usually the rider's fault. When people say to us in surprise, "I can do it too—thanks to such a nice horse!" we take it as a compliment because we made that nice horse the way he is.

## Conclusion

A horse only learns something when it benefits him directly. If he learns something that you do not want—for example, rearing—then he is doing it because it benefits *him*. Rearing is used to avoid work, and when that happens, your horse has become the leader. As long as your horse is the boss, riding is a dangerous pastime.

The Question and Answer method is one of the most important training strategies we have to control and "shape" the horse. Question and Answer training consists of Four Steps: Action, Pressure, Reaction, and Reward. It is a positive method because "learning" occurs at the moment the rider removes *pressure* because the horse is giving him the desired *reaction* (the Target Behavior); as a result, the horse associates performing the Target Behavior with something positive: his *reward*.

According to this principle, a horse does not learn to go forward because the rider is using his leg but because he has learned this leg pressure *stops immediately* when he goes forward. Thus, the horse is not going forward to do *you* a favor but to do *himself* a favor by getting rid of the pressure.

As discussed (p. 83), giving treats, scratching the crest, and removing pressure are *primary* rewards. Remember, you can also use a *secondary* reward, such as verbal praise. When you do, you have to regularly "maintain" the effect of the secondary reward, which is accomplished by giving the secondary reward and primary reward together on a regular basis. The act of association makes the secondary reward just as effective as the primary reward.

Always keep the Six Basic Rules in mind when training with the Question and Answer method. When your horse still does not understand what you want, look at yourself to figure out where you went wrong. Pat Parelli, the well-known American horse trainer, compares the horse to a computer: it does exactly what you ask but not always what you want. In other words, when your horse does something other than you want, you must always ask yourself if you inadvertently pushed the wrong "button!"

# Tineke on Training with the Question and Answer Method

IT IS FASCINATING TO study the training systems that top riders use, and this is why Imke and I have trained regularly with Anky van Grunsven and Sjef Janssen since 1998. They train using a refined Question and Answer game. Sjef was able to develop his training system by working with one of the most talented riders in the history of the sport.

Given that I was trained in the systematic, classical school, I first had to start thinking in a different way. Of course, this classical foundation was not suddenly deemed worthless, but I certainly needed to train differently—with more creativity and more variety. I had to stop using my leg "just like that" but instead give a touch with my calves, two touches, or even more. I had to think about all the aids I had always just given.

I also had to try to simplify my aids and use a separate aid for every exercise. My aids became more refined; I stopped doing things just because I had always done them and started doing things because

they had an effect. That was not so simple. Even when I wanted to do something differently, I could not just do it. At first, my body did not do what I wanted because my motor skills were trained to do things another way. It took thousands of repetitions to stop using the old aids and to learn the new ones, especially since I had to learn to give these aids with unconscious-competence, in other words, on automatic pilot.

I remember a discussion about clucking to my horse. According to Sjef, I did that far too often, so there was no benefit to it. I had to cluck sparingly, "reserving" clucks for when I really needed them, such as a transition to passage from the walk. Indeed, I really needed to use all my aids more sparingly.

The concept works as follows: aid the horse once and do not repeat the aid if your horse responds. Let him maintain the exercise by himself. Then, allow your legs to hang relaxed and just make sure you are not hindering the horse. Apply another aid only when you want him to do something else. I had to

become much more consistent at giving aids. Slowly but surely, training became a far more aware Question and Answer game.

Of course, we also started training our horses in other positions: deeper, longer, rounder, and shorter. We initially did not ride our horses much with a very deep neck position. I often found it difficult to ride them "up" again—in a show frame—after training them to go deeper for a while. But that was an old shortcoming because long before I started training with Sjef, I would get comments on my tests from judges about my horse being "behind the vertical." That continued until I understood that position control depends on tempo control. When I got my horses better to my leg and lighter in my hand, position control also became much easier.

What is the main difference in Sjef and Anky's approach? For one, you always have to start with your horse. There are many individual differences between horses. In the end, your horse's forward desire should no longer come from you and your legs but from the horse himself. You have to teach your horse to think forward.

I think an important principle is to avoid making something difficult when it can be done easily. For instance, using four different actions to do a canter transition is confusing and practically impossible. Doing a downward transition from the trot to the walk by driving the horse to the hand is not logical because then you are using two opposing aids at the same time. You also do not want to step on the "gas" and the "brake" at the same time—this only leads to "riding with the hand brake on." For this reason, Anky and Sjef rarely tell their students that they "must ride the horse to the hand."

In my opinion, I believe the proof that Anky and Sjef are on the right path is mainly evident in the enjoyment that Anky's horses display in their work. This is because Anky keeps her horses fresh by continually surprising them and because she is super quick with her perfect hands and her brilliant leg aids. Anky plays with pressure and relaxation like no other.

*Imke's rides in Athens brought her more than applause and an Olympic certificate. She also collected "feel information," which should prove invaluable. This "feel" is her compass and she will continue to build on it in her training. In addition, she got a close-up look at how the phenomenal rider Anky van Grunsven prepared for her second Olympic gold medal win.*

CHAPTER 6

# Riding with "Feel"

## What Is Rider "Feel?"

Rider "feel" is the last link in communication between rider and horse. It is a connecting feeling that goes out from the rider and is answered by the horse. Richard Weis compares this to two partners who are dancing the tango and implicitly are one. In this example, the rider is the lead dance partner.

Rider feel happens when you have sufficient knowledge and a lot of practical experience. This is why "you only learn to ride by riding" is such a well-known saying in the horse world. It is the automatic reciprocity between rider and horse that occurs when your horse does what you ask without any resistance.

Imke had great feel in the Grand Prix at the Athens Olympics, where she competed on Lancet. When she came out of the ring, Tineke said: "Well ridden!" to which Imke answered: "I didn't have to ride at all; it happened by itself." The communication between horse and rider was so fine-tuned that both operated on "automatic pilot," so to speak. In chapter 3, we referred to this as *unconscious-competence.* How do you achieve it?

You also learned in chapter 3 that we must have goals in order to achieve something: an end goal, long-range and mid-range goals, and a short-term goal. Let us start with the end goal.

You understand your horse, and he understands you. Your body gives the aids automatically; you do not have to think about them. Your horse reacts immediately. He thinks with you. If you set a certain tempo, your horse maintains that tempo on his own. You give an aid to begin an exercise, and your horse completes the exercise on his own. When you want to change tempo or direction of travel, your new aids go through immediately.

If something in the surroundings attracts your horse's attention, you subconsciously feel it coming before it happens. Without thinking about it, you give your horse a few half-halts and make sure his attention stays focused on you. Your automatic pilot gives the aids, and your horse's automatic pilot carries them out. The two of you become one. You feel bonded. Riding is suddenly very comfortable.

The end goal just described is based on your horse's total trust in you. Your horse trusts you and feels safe under your leadership. Your horse opens himself physically and mentally. He feels like a part of you. This

Imke's achievements with Lancet at the Athens Olympics provided her with important information about feel. The optimum rider feel from those Olympics is stored in her automatic pilot. Her rider feel is the compass that enables her to find the right path to the end goal: a horse that "opens" himself to the rider.

feeling is actually rare; that is why we call it the end goal. However, if you have achieved it once, you will never forget it. This is also why it was so terrible for Imke when Lancet was sold after the Athens Olympics. She felt as though she lost a part of herself. Fortunately, Imke still has the memory of that optimum feel with Lancet. She has saved it in her automatic pilot, so to speak.

When she started riding Sunrise, it became easier for Imke to reproduce that good feeling after a time. She had a better feel for what she was working toward. Imke's Olympic experiences likely made an important contribution to the development of her rider feel.

Many top riders have this same experience. When they get one top horse with which they can experience this optimum feeling, they can recapture it more easily with other horses. Their rider feel is clearly the compass that enables them to find the right path to the end goal: a horse that opens himself to the rider.

### The Ten Systematic Training Phases

Riders often expect results too quickly. This is a most common mistake. If Imke had strived for the end goal too fast with her new horses, specifically the optimum feel she had achieved with Lancet, she likely would have come to a quick standstill with Sunrise. She had to set new, smart goals for the midterm and the short-term. Where do I want to be next year; what does that mean for the next several months; and how do I work my horse tomorrow?

After Athens, Imke and Tineke developed a plan, outlining each phase of the way. In the end, everything went faster than they had expected. This demonstrates once again that the slow way is usually the fastest way in the end. Furthermore, it is better to adjust your goals in a positive way because things progressed faster than you had planned than it is to be forced to take a step back. The slow way, which consists of phases that are easily achievable individually, gives you motivation.

Of course, training must stay challenging. By "the slow way," we mean that you do not start doing all kinds of complicated exercises too quickly but first ensure that you have good basics. The basics are primarily aimed at relaxing the horse and focusing his attention on the rider's aids. This applies both to long-term planning and daily training.

### Our Training System

We work with our horses the "slow way." This slow way consists of logical "training phases," each of which must be systematically completed. If you have carefully read the previous chapters, you now know the basic conditions and principles. You know your horse; you know yourself; you

ride with an independent seat; and you use the Question and Answer training system. Now, you have to further develop your horse using your rider feel as a compass.

Without rider feel, you cannot develop your horse. We will try to explain the progression of that development process. You may find our explanation a bit complicated at points, which is quite understandable. Although we work daily with ordinary amateur riders, the Academy is now also involved with the sport at the Olympic level. This may mean that certain parts of training seem practically unattainable. Even so, we think that most parts are workable for average riders and their horses. After all, we see this in practice at our training clinics.

Tineke always says that you need lots of "flight hours" to develop your rider feel. You have to physically experience what is happening with your horse through lots of practice, preferably under a good instructor. Your horse is the only standard in your training. If he develops in a positive way, you are on the right path.

When you have gained enough practical experience that you can feel your horse, you can go to work. This work must be systematic, which means that you cannot proceed with Phase 2 if Phase 1 is not yet complete.

On the following pages we outline the Ten Systematic Phases of training:

*Phase 1 of training: give a new horse plenty of time to become accustomed to you (see p. 104). This phase applies both to young horses and new horses, such as Sunrise, whom Imke took over from Tineke in the fall of 2004. The position that Sunrise is demonstrating in this photo is the goal of Phase 1 where you try to let your horse find the low, long neck position on his own, without using your hands. If your horse lowers his head of his own initiative, he is signaling his physical and mental relaxation. Then you can start working.*

### Ten Training Phases

1 Give a young or new horse the chance to get used to you and relax before you begin.
2 Train tempo control: refine the reaction to your leg aids and rein aids.
3 Apply your leg aids and rein aids separately.
4 Teach your horse to "give" to a "resisting" hand.
5 Develop the game of Question and Answer through tempo changes.
6 Invite your horse to "let his head fall" (first stage in position control).
7 Work on athletic development by shortening and lengthening your horse (second stage of position control).
8 Work on removing all blockages.
9 Allow elevation and collection to happen naturally.
10 Strive for your horse to "open" to you physically and mentally.

*Phase 1:   Give a young or new horse a chance to get used to you and relax before you begin.*

Every rider and every horse need time to become familiar with one another. This applies mainly to young horses but also goes for more experienced combinations. Even Imke and Sunrise first had to get used to each other. Lancet, a "macho" stallion, had a completely different personality than the hot-tempered and willful prima donna, Sunrise. Both horses are sensitive, but Lancet was less dominant than Sunrise. Initially, Sunrise could drive Imke to exasperation. It was quite difficult for her to gain dominance over Sunrise without damaging the mare's confidence. To achieve that, Imke had to start at the beginning again, just like everyone else.

The process of *habituation* should be handled sensibly (p. 79). The rider begins very carefully—certainly with a young horse—and exerts just a little influence over him. Initially, you leave a lot to your horse and later, slowly increase your influence.

Study your horse during this phase. Your horse tells you what you can do in training. Learn how to put yourself in his place and listen to him.

When your horse trusts you, he can be relaxed from different positions. To this end, the long-and-low, forward-downward positioned head and neck is an important basic principle. Wait until your horse takes this position himself; do not ask for it. When he trusts you, he will lower his head on his own. There are more reasons for using this approach:

1 In prey-animal psychology (Voest), a low head-neck position that we describe as "forward and downward" is associated with safety and relaxation (grazing, drinking, and resting).
2 A lowered neck position also demonstrates that the horse is focused on his rider and therefore less easily distracted.
3 A low neck position is another sign of physical relaxation. According to horse anatomy (Van Weeren, Slijper), a low head-neck position creates an upward arch of the back in which the dorsal spinous processes spread farther apart and the back muscles relax.

4  A horse that lowers his neck is also more enjoyable for the rider; he "loosens" his back more easily and therefore allows the rider to sit more comfortably. A horse in this position gives himself over to the rider physically and mentally, as though he were saying: "Okay, just tell me what we're going to do now." This also happens because the horse feels more comfortable in the deep position.

Do not ride your horse too short in the neck during this phase; instead invite him to relax. The rider does not yet try to control the horse's position. The lowered position must come entirely from the horse. Much later, at your initiative, you can alternate between lengthening and shortening the horse. Then, you stretch the horse, trying to find his limit at times and then relaxing again, something that is frequently used in the training methods of human athletes. But we are not dealing with that now! Shortening and lengthening is a process that takes years, in which the athlete keeps making small advancements. It is not unusual for an experienced gymnast to do a split, but such a movement can seriously damage the muscles of a beginner. Muscles have to become accustomed to the training process step by step over a long period.

*Tineke takes Sunrise over a small jump. Work over cavaletti and small jumps is good for gymnastic development and provides necessary variety. When Sunrise came to the Academy, we needed to incorporate a lot of different types of schooling and fun in her training: she needed to enjoy her work again. Cavaletti work and schooling jumps allow your horse to find his own way to the long, low neck position. This position is the foundation of your training.*

*Phase 2 of training is tempo control, the most important exercise with a young horse and the most important exercise through the Olympic level. When you do not have control over the "gas" and "brake," you cannot teach your horse to "give" to the bit, and position control is impossible. A leg aid must be followed immediately by the horse going forward (Reaction), after which you soften your hand and allow your legs to hang passively (Reward). You must teach your horse to maintain the requested tempo on his own, without any supporting aids. The galloping track or riding on the trail are both ideal places to test your horse's reaction to your leg aids, and teach him to "think" forward.*

**You must be able to "step on the gas" or "use the brakes" whenever you want. As long as you do not have total control over tempo, the horse cannot really "give" to the bit while he is moving.**

*Phase 2: Train tempo control: refine the reaction to your leg aids and rein aids.*

Once you and your horse are accustomed to one another, *tempo control* is your first assignment. To achieve something, you first have to make your horse very obedient to leg and rein aids. He must learn that *you* determine the tempo (speed). You must be able to step on the "gas" or the "brakes" whenever you want; otherwise, riding is not fun at all and sometimes even outright dangerous. To decrease the tempo by increasing rein pressure requires daily training. Increasing pressure on both reins means "whoa." The leg aid for the "gas" is a touch with both legs.

We begin practicing this fairly soon with young horses, primarily in the walk. We start carefully, with very small aids and few tempo changes; later, we slowly ask for more. Then, we do the same in the trot. Your horse's balance develops as a result of the aids becoming refined, which helps him to control his tempo. When the horse is on the aids, he goes forward immediately and increases his tempo from your leg aid. Conversely, he slows his tempo and reduces his speed from your rein aid. The "gas" and the "brake" give you control over speed. You also teach your horse to wait for the next aid without "shutting off the motor," which means you teach him to continue at the same tempo until he gets another aid from you.

As long as you do not have total control over tempo, your horse cannot "give" to the bit while in motion. In this situation, you are reduced to trying to get him to give to the bit from a halt—something that many riders do; however, this method carries the risk of riding just with your hands. The quality of giving to the bit resides in the interplay between the leg aid and the rein aid, which you simply cannot get with a horse that is standing still.

Your horse must learn to always *think* forward, even when he is standing still. His "motor" must not shut off because then it has to be restarted; you can ride off much easier with a running motor.

For this reason, tempo control is an essential concept of horsemanship. When the aids come through well and tempo control is optimum, the gas and the brakes come so close together that a brilliant sequence between both aids is ultimately created. This is when we can really "shift gears": ride transitions and make adjustments, with submission to the bit and, ultimately, collection as the natural result. But more about that later.

*Phase 3: Apply your leg aids and rein aids separately.*

Some trainers advocate using your driving aids and rein aids at the same time. Proponents of this method say that "you have to ride to the hand, which puts the horse between the leg and bit, so to speak." We think this is an unfortunate image because we too often see riders who "step on the gas" while "holding the hand brake." In our lessons, we keep the driving aids and the rein aids separate.

Rein aids and driving aids can hinder one another. Let's say you touch your horse with your legs to go more forward (*action*), and he does not

RIDE HORSES WITH AWARENESS AND FEEL

*react*, so you give a stronger aid (*pressure*). Finally, you get a *reaction* and the horse flies forward. Your first reflex is to grab the reins. This happens almost automatically when you do not have an independent seat. The sudden forward motion of your horse makes you fall backward, so you unconsciously seek support from the reins. This is how a good reaction

*Tempo control plays an important role in most parts of the dressage test. Imke is pictured riding an extended canter on Sunrise. We can see the extension very well, but if Sunrise does not "come back" from a light aid at the end of the diagonal, then Imke will receive a low score for the movement. Her braking aid consists of a combination of more pressure on the reins and a deeper seat. Some riders can slow their horses down just with their seat. This slowing aid must clearly differ from the aid used to ask a horse to give to the bit. Top riders constantly do transitions and tempo changes. They use these exercises to further improve tempo control and fine-tune the aids.*

from the horse (going forward) is punished instead of rewarded. As a result, the principle of Action, Pressure, Reaction, and Reward is changed into the principle of Action, Pressure, Reaction, and Punishment.

Instead of falling backward and pulling on the reins, you have to go forward with the horse and "give" the reins. This is how you reward the horse for his forward reaction and ensure that this positive reaction is stored in his memory.

To teach a horse how to slow down, use only rein aids—definitely no leg aids at first. Exert pressure on the bit through the reins, and decrease that pressure as soon as the horse goes slower.

Ensure that the gas and brakes work in such a way that you can determine the exact tempo you want to ride. Tempo control is the most important point on which you should continue to focus.

We stated earlier that a horse will not give to the bit without good tempo control. Riders often do not realize that they are riding at a speed determined by the horse. We sometimes ask our students: "Is this the tempo you want?" They often look at us with surprise and say: "I really don't know!" In that case, they first have to realize that they do not have control over the tempo—the horse does.

Tempo control is a funda-
mental concept in dressage.
You must be very clear with
your leg aids and rein aids.
For this reason, make sure
that you learn to apply your
leg aids and rein aids separately. Otherwise, they will
work against each other,
which can lead to confusion
and tension.

*Phase 4:   Teach your horse to "give" to a "resisting" hand.*

Many riders do not know the difference between the rein aid of the *restraining* hand ("slowing aid") and the rein aid of the *resisting* hand ("giving" to the bit aid). Tineke thinks this is one of the most difficult things to explain clearly because it is about feel. However, she often explains it as follows:

*"You ask totally different reactions from your horse with a 'restraining' versus 'resisting' hand. The Target Behavior of a restraining hand is for your horse to go slower. The Target Behavior of a resisting hand is for your horse to 'give' to the bit—his jaw relaxes and he chews softly on the bit, a sign of relaxation. Horses that trust one another show this in the wild by making chewing motions and licking."*

You have to use different *actions* to teach your horse to keep his *reactions* to these aids separate. In other words, your horse must immediately understand which aid you are giving: the restraining rein aid or the resisting aid for giving to the bit. Fortunately, horses only need small differences between aids to keep them separate; but you must make these differences clear *and* apply them consistently.

With a young horse, always teach him the meaning of the restraining rein aid first. Once he understands this, you can start teaching him to give to a resisting hand. To slow the horse, apply clear pressure to both reins; use more rein pressure until he slows down. Most riders combine this rein aid with a deeper seat. Use gravity to tell your horse that he needs to slow down. Maintain the pressure until the tempo changes; then immediately soften your hand and lighten your seat.

Exactly how you combine the rein aid and seat aid is not that important, as long as you apply the combination consistently and your horse understands it. You also have to teach your horse to maintain that slower tempo until you give the next aid, for example, a leg aid to go more forward. If you want to go even slower, then give another restraining aid, followed by relaxation when your horse obeys.

The resisting rein aid is just slightly different. In principle, it is a smaller aid than the restraining aid. The rein pressure is less constant; the hand is more "playful." You also do not deepen your seat, as with the restraining aid. Your hand action is like that of the rubber rings on side reins when they are attached from the saddle to the bit. Feel as though your hand is squeezing out a sponge that immediately is filled with water again. Remember, never pull back!

When your horse relaxes his jaw and mouth, he gets lighter in the reins, and your hand must soften immediately. When your horse gets stronger against the bit, use a stronger rein aid.

Your horse must maintain the same tempo when you apply the resisting aid. If you need to apply a leg aid sometime during this process

*Imke asks Sunrise to give to the bit from a "resisting" (as opposed to "restraining" for slowing down) hand. Do not start working on this if you do not yet have tempo control because tempo must always come first. The rein aid for giving to the bit is comparable to the action of a side-rein with a rubber ring. Wait until your horse relaxes his jaw and softly chews on the bit. When he does this, relax your hand immediately.*

because the horse slows down, do not apply the hand and leg aid together but apply them quickly and well-timed, one after the other.

Start by practicing the resisting aid for giving to the bit in the gait that is easiest for the horse, which is often the walk or the trot. Some riders practice the resisting hand at the halt; however, doing so has a disadvantage that we have already discussed: using too much hand, which causes the horse to stop thinking forward over time. A forward-thinking horse is a prerequisite for giving to the bit.

Later, your horse must be able to respond to your resisting aid for giving to the bit in the most challenging situations. You want to use this aid to teach your horse to relax and concentrate on you under all circumstances, which is done by building on this exercise.

*Phase 5:   Develop the Question and Answer game using tempo changes.*
If the basic prerequisites are present—namely, *tempo control* and *giving to the bit*—you can keep refining communication with your horse through the Question and Answer game. Given that we have focused quite a bit on the rein aids, some may get the wrong impression and think that riding is "hand work." In fact, the opposite is true: "leg work" is just as important in riding! Most riders get stuck because their horses are not sufficiently "in front of" the leg.

**Your horse must recognize the difference between the *restraining* aid for slowing down and the *resisting* aid for giving to the bit. To reduce speed, use more rein pressure and sit a bit deeper in the saddle until your horse slows down. The aid for giving to the bit is smaller than the restraining aid and is applied without deepening the seat. Your hand action is like that of the rubber rings on side reins when they are attached from the saddle to the bit. Feel as though your hand is squeezing out a sponge that immediately gets filled with water again. *Never pull back.***

When you do not get the right response from the horse to your leg aid, you can only apply that aid more strongly when you have learned to give *differentiated* leg aids. Examples of such include a soft leg aid (calf), a slightly stronger aid (calf and heel), a yet stronger aid (spur), and a double leg aid (two well-timed touches of the inner lower leg or spur). Differentiated aids allow you to increase the pressure according to the training principle of Action, Pressure, Reaction, and Reward. A less sensitive horse may require a stronger leg or spur, a triple aid, or even a touch with the whip so that the horse is challenged to react to the aid. We prefer to ride without a dressage whip since it is not allowed in competition. Most horses can be trained quite well without a whip.

When the horse's reaction meets the Target Behavior, then remove the pressure immediately. It is usually not a bad thing when a young horse that still does not listen to the leg well, goes too forward or picks up the canter. Praise him for *increasing* the tempo and going more forward. This also has to happen with a great deal of feel: consciously feel that you are aiding your horse the way you want.

In between, continue to ensure that your legs hang completely relaxed and do not bother the horse—this is a basic principle. The more still your legs are, the better the horse understands when you aid him lightly. If your legs are always moving, your horse will stop feeling your driving leg. The more quiet the leg, the better a soft leg aid comes through. The reaction to a leg aid or rein aid should be like electricity: when you flip on a light switch, the light goes on immediately and stays on. Therefore, every aid must have such an effect! In addition, you must ensure that your aids become more refined and small, yet still generate this same effect.

*Tineke asks her students many questions when she teaches them; consequently they learn to think about their own training. One of her most frequent is: "Is this the tempo you want?" Her students often look surprised and say: "I really don't know." In this case, the tempo is probably not determined by the rider but by the horse!*

When your horse understands the brake and the gas well, then you can "shift gears"—in other words, ride tempo changes. The goal of tempo changes is to refine the aids and increase your *action* skills and your horse's *reaction* skills, too. You can use the driving and restraining aids in very quick succession.

Classical horsemanship uses the term "half-halt." Using the gas and brakes in quick succession energizes your horse. Every half-halt is initiated by a forward reaction to the leg that generates speed and more activity, followed, a fraction of a second later, by a rein aid to ask the horse to come back.

Even when tempo changes are greatly refined, experienced riders sometimes run into problems, such as the horse running out from under the rider or coming back too much, which causes the connection and balance to be lost. Tempo changes must be repeated and refined whenever the horse assumes a tempo that you do not want. You *always* set the horse's tempo.

Playing with the tempo is *the* basic principle for training communication. Doing tempo changes and half-halts are tests that reveal whether or not *you* are in control. You ask the horse to concentrate on you. You apply your leg and receive the horse with the reins, the effects of which are his extra attention, energy, and relaxation. This is the most important concentration exercise and a very good balancing one, too.

*Phase 6: Invite your horse to "let his head fall"—first stage of position control.*

In Phase 1, you worked on inviting your horse to drop his head entirely of his own free will, which did not involve any real position control. Now you work on getting him to drop his head and neck whenever you ask.

As stated earlier, you can only position a horse deeper when he has learned how to give to the bit from a resisting hand. Then you can ask him to "let his head fall," which means that he drops his head and neck to a lower position upon your request. Even this exercise can only be done correctly through the Question and Answer method. You have to keep testing your horse to check his proficiency at this game.

The hand acts like a flexible side rein. It "breathes" but does not pull back. Your horse must learn to react to the hand by relaxing his jaw and chewing on the bit softly. You can position your horse a bit rounder by building on this aid. Remember that asking your horse to give to the bit or positioning him deeper has nothing to do with "pulling a horse round," whether or not done with the aid of draw reins. Force does not belong in this method nor does it belong in any other method of dressage. The training process is a subtle one, in which progress is made step by step. Also, try to keep your horse from *leaning* on your hands. When your horse gives to the bit, the "hand brake" is released; the blockages are gone from his body; and the movement can flow from back to front.

If you ask a horse to give to the bit or come deeper, make sure that he

Playing with tempo changes focuses the horse's concentration on you. Ride tempo changes and half-halts by "stepping on the gas" with your legs and then "braking" with your reins, alternating these aids in short succession. This exercise energizes your horse more. The rein contact becomes lighter because your horse is carrying himself. The goal of tempo changes is to refine the aids and increase your Action skills and the Reaction skills of your horse. Furthermore, it is a good balancing exercise.

does not go "behind the bit," thus avoiding your aids by dropping the contact and not reacting to the leg. Do not position a young horse as deep and round as you might a 12-year-old Grand Prix horse but do vary his head position as soon as you have control over the tempo. Position your horse a bit deeper and then a bit higher again. This control over varying the head-neck position should be developed further step by step. When we do these position exercises with young horses, we also do continuous tempo changes to check that the horse's reaction to our leg stays sharp enough. This prepares him for the more difficult exercises we will ask of him later in training.

It is difficult to say at what point we start asking more of a horse. In this respect, dressage is custom work; we do not have a standard model.

*Among the horse's various "positions," in our training system, forward-and-downward is always the basic one you return to. In Phase 1, you let the horse find the position himself. In Phase 6, which is the first stage of position control, you teach the horse to "let his head fall" at your request. In Phase 7, the second stage of position control, you alternate making your horse short and long in the deeper position. Then the true gymnastic work begins where you develop your horse, work his "blockages" away, and strengthen his muscles.*

*Training Phase 1: Sunrise willingly "lets her head fall."*

*Training Phase 6: Imke uses a low hand to ask Sunrise to lower her head.*

RIDE HORSES WITH AWARENESS AND FEEL

This, too, involves a bit of rider feel. The horse tells you when he is able to do something; when he is supple and strong enough in the back, then it happens "naturally," as it were.

*Phase 7:    Work on athletic development—second stage of position control.*
You now ask a bit more from your horse. In Phase 1, we patiently waited until he lowered his neck position from his own will as a sign that he trusts us. In Phase 6, he learned to drop his neck in response to an aid. You may now proceed a step further, under the strict condition that you have already mastered tempo control. You will now teach your horse to alternately become short and long, which is an important step in his further athletic development.

Actually, we think that it is helpful for riders to regularly work with a professional sports trainer to experience the effects of developing their own body. Development takes place by systematically moving your limits. You exert yourself but always make sure that you recover again. You search for your limits and then relax again. Effort and relaxation are two concepts that are bound together in the training progression of an athlete.

The words "top athlete" as relating to the horse are relatively new to the sport, and there are still classical "fundamentalists" who find the FEI's implementation of the expression "happy athlete" in its rules very inappropriate.

For us, the horse's athletic development is an important hallmark of our new, Academy Bartels "total method." Tineke used the words "total method" in a December 2005 interview with the Dutch equestrian magazine *de Hoefslag,* in which she described her development as a rider. By implementing a better training system that focuses more on the details of psychological and athletic development, she was able to facilitate a much more complete training of the horse. In the past, we often saw horses that could passage or piaffe well but that were not all-around athletes.

The FEI did not simply conjure up the term "happy athlete" out of thin air; the term was founded on a clear vision: the desire for a completely gymnasticized horse that thinks with the rider, a horse that does not do his work like a machine but takes pleasure in his work. Of course, this also means taking into consideration the great differences in talent between horses. It is a challenge for the trainer to actualize a horse's optimum athletic development within his physical and mental capacities. "I think our way of training creates top athletes," asserts Tineke.

It is a fantastic experience to develop a horse into a top athlete and feel that he is almost a part of you. Tineke and Imke together have trained more than 10 horses to international Grand Prix level. Some were ordinary horses, but in recent years, there have been increasingly better horses that were also better trained. The nice feeling that Tineke and Imke have enjoyed with horses such as Lancet and Sunrise is something that they previously thought was impossible. That feeling is partly due to the talent of these horses but mainly due to the training method.

A horse must first learn to give to the bit from a resisting hand before you can ask him to "let his head fall." The control necessary to vary the head-neck position is developed step by step. When you do these position exercises, you must also ride continuous tempo changes to check that the horse's reaction to your leg stays sharp. The process is a subtle one, in which progress is made incrementally.

*Varying position and tempo*—long and short, high and deep, fast and slow—plays a major role in this method. These are key concepts. Of course, there are also challenges and you have to learn how to deal with them. How is it that some riders can put their horses "deep" and then transition immediately to an upright showing position—with the horse's nose just in front of the vertical—yet other riders cannot? Riders who can accomplish this, first of all, have their horses unconditionally forward and "in front of" the leg. As we've said, position control is the result of tempo control, and *tempo control is a basic requirement.*

At the Academy, we adjust our hand position to make it even clearer to the horse what head position we want from him. We make a consistent distinction between a somewhat wider and lower hand position for riding a horse round and the correct position for showing with hands above the withers and the horse's nose in front of the vertical. This distinction allows the snaffle-elbow line to remain straight in both the deep and upright positions.

If you cannot control your horse's tempo and he does not react quickly to the leg, you will be unable to influence his head-neck position. For this reason, you should not begin riding your horse deep and round if you do not yet have tempo control. Furthermore, deep and round riding is not equally appropriate for every horse. In other words, always evaluate the effect on the individual horse.

### Phase 8: Work on removing all blockages.

What is a blockage? According to Tineke, a block exists when a horse holds himself tight somewhere in his body, for which there may be mental or physical reasons.

First, we will focus on the mental reasons. Some horses lose their confidence in a particular position, situation, or exercise. As a result, they stiffen and get "tight" in their body. For example, Sunrise used to panic when Tineke wanted to practice flying changes. Perhaps Sunrise had a bad past experience, the memories of which led to blockages in her body. It took a long time before Sunrise got over her fear of flying changes. It took a step-by-step process that lasted almost two years.

Blocks due to physical reasons originate from discomfort or pain. When a horse experiences pain, it tenses its muscles. A horse is many times stronger than its rider, so you have no chance of breaking through your horse's muscle tension by using force or harshness. You can best deal with these blockages by approaching them as a personal trainer or physical therapist would: you find appropriate gymnastic exercises for your horse's problem. Do these exercises very patiently and increase their difficulty incrementally. This is how you make your horse gradually more supple and stronger.

Blockages somehow interrupt and interfere with the energy that you generated from the horse's hindquarters. You can imagine this energy streaming like a wave that must come through 100 percent to achieve

If you cannot control your horse's tempo, you cannot influence his head-neck position. If you cannot play with your horse's position, you cannot develop your horse athletically. Correct athletic development makes your horse a "happy athlete," the most important hallmark of the Academy Bartels training method described in this book.

*Working on removing "blockages"
is a job for experts. Begin this work
only when you have mastered all
the preceding phases and thoroughly
analyzed your horse. The work should
take place under good supervision.
Tineke and Imke spend a lot of
time analyzing blocks. What causes
them? If the cause is physical, they
usually call the vet. If the cause is
psychological, they sometimes consult
with a behavioral expert, like Emiel
Voest. Most importantly, however,
is that the rider and trainer learn
to "read" the horse based on his
reactions to determine if they are
on the right track.*

optimum performance. Blockages cannot usually be seen but are certainly felt. Removing physical and mental blockages is most important in order to develop a horse into a top athlete. Playing with the energy by lengthening and shortening, changing the tempo, and varying the neck position ultimately leads to a horse that becomes supple—vertebra by vertebra. Good training "massages" all the blockages out of the horse, and only then can he develop optimally.

The spectacular movement of top horses is not usually a product of nature alone. The training process is also instrumental in their development, the result of which is complete "looseness" and suppleness. Riders feel this looseness mainly in lightness of contact in combination with good balance and absolute obedience to the smallest possible leg aids. We have experienced this process in our own horses in the past years. Since we started training with Anky and Sjef, our method has become more focused on lightness and on horses that—without blocks—carry themselves and no longer need the support of the reins. We assure you

The reason for varying tempo, length, and position—making the horse more supple—is to remove all blockages. A horse has a block when it holds itself tight somewhere in its body. Removing blocks allows you to develop your horse into an athlete. At the same time, ensure your horse's mental development by giving a lot of attention to variety and reward.

that riding is much more comfortable for us now than it was in the past. It requires less effort, and we are convinced that our horses enjoy their work more. This is also due to the attention given to variety when schooling—the horses never know what is coming next.

### Phase 9:   Allow elevation and collection to happen naturally.

If your horse reacts to the "gas" and the "brake," and you have tempo and head-and-neck position control, you can start thinking about collection. The concept of "collection" is quite often thought of as "driving from behind and holding in front." This is wrong (see p. 106). Almost everyone has his own idea of the concept of collection, but achieving the ideal state of collection is not easy. Developing collection is a long process.

It takes many years to make a horse stronger through development of his muscles and increasing his mental willingness and understanding. We seldom say "collect your horse" during our lessons at the Academy because when collection becomes the main goal, the result too often is pushing and pulling. Asking for collection tends to make you use your hands and create too strong a connection with the mouth, which blocks self-carriage and impulsion. It also leads to a "busy" seat and aids, and your upper body moves too much. All this put together creates a tense situation in which collection can never happen.

Therefore, when you focus solely on collection, you will probably get just the opposite of what you want because your attempts will hinder relaxation and giving to the bit. Giving to the bit is always a part of collection. Collection is the result of step-by-step training where the basic principles are confirmed, every day, year after year. If these basic points are correct and the horse is unconditionally on the aids, you can then say that collection "just happens."

Despite the fact that collected strides are shorter than working strides, the collected gaits are more expressive. The horse's neck becomes more upright through a better connection with and greater activity of the hind legs. Science shows us the importance of tempo control and great activity in collection, and we can apply this information in practice.

In the early 1990s, Professor Hilary Clayton did a study on collection at the University of Utrecht in the Netherlands. During that time, Tineke brought her Grand Prix horses to Professor Clayton several times to do piaffe and other movements on a scale that registered the weight of each footfall. Her research findings were published in *The Equine Veterinary Supplement on Equine Locomotion* in 1994.

Clayton's scientific research has practical value for riders because she concluded that though a horse's average speed progressively *decreases* as it is collected more, its energy *increases*. If you try to only create small, slow strides because you think this is how your horse collects, the process will definitely end in disaster: you need a high degree of energy to create faster, quicker movements. A low degree of energy leads to slow movements that don't "flow"; hence, your horse will lack sufficient balance, suppleness, submission to the bit, and purity in his gaits. You have then achieved the opposite of collection.

A horse in correct collection indeed moves more slowly, but the rhythm of the gait stays regular and his movement becomes more powerful and sharper. The collected gaits are relatively "expensive" with respect to energy compared to the working, medium, and extended gaits, according to Clayton. Although the collected gaits are the slowest, they require a great deal of energy—a point to remember.

*Phase 10:  Strive for your horse to "open" to you physically and mentally.*
Your rider feel is your compass when training. The horse's development tells you when you are on the right path, which you can see in his muscle development and notice in his willingness to react to increasingly finer and smaller aids.

It is difficult for an outsider to judge muscle development in the top of the neck and hindquarters, as some horses are naturally well-muscled and others are not. However, if you follow a specific horse over time, you can see precisely if his rider is on the right path.

This is how we can name the jumper and dressage riders who make their horses nicer and those who do not. Actually, a judge should also take this into consideration in his or her evaluation. The fact is that dressage is about *the development of natural abilities* and to a lesser extent about natural talent.

To what extent does the new training method encompass other objectives in addition to the classical basic principles? Most objectives are the same. It is often a matter of semantics. In the German Training Scale, *Durchlässigkeit* is the final goal. People have tried for years (in many languages) to come up with a good translation for this word. We have chosen the word *open.*

A horse that *opens* himself physically because his back is relaxed and connected with his hindquarters—all his blockages are gone—can be comfortable ridden. Runners know the same feeling, called a "runner's high," when the body operates on "automatic pilot." The athlete may say to himself: "My body is running; I don't have to do anything. It feels great."

He also opens to you mentally because when he feels safe with you—as a herd animal and team player—he will cooperate.

An "open" horse offers himself to you. You can lengthen and shorten him as well as extend and collect him like an accordion, if so desired. You can develop him athletically, and through this, work on removing all blockages. Once you achieve this, you no longer have to worry about teaching specific movements or asking for collection. These happen on their own.

We know this sounds like a fairy tale. Many young riders have a hard time believing top riders when they say that they spend 90 percent of their time on the basics and athletic development, but it is the truth! Even

When you make collection the main goal and focus on it too quickly, the end result is often just "pushing and pulling"—you achieve the *opposite* what you are striving for in the horse. When the horse's blockages disappear and he is unconditionally on the aids, collection "just happens."

The end goal of our training is for the horse to "open" himself to the rider and develop mentally and athletically, and through this, all blockages disappear and the horse feels safe with his rider. Horse and rider then become one. An open horse is evident by the development of his muscles and gaits, and by his willingness to respond to increasingly finer and smaller aids.

collection happens by itself when the basics are good. Collection is actually the rider and horse coming into balance. *Balance is a key concept*—by which we mean *mental* and *physical* balance.

## The Structure of Daily Training

Your daily training is based on the same logical order that we described previously. First, determine where your horse is in the phase-by-phase process just outlined, and which points you want to work on. However, even with a Grand Prix horse, daily work starts by going through a basic sequence: first relaxation; then tempo control; then position control; and finally, gymnastic development. Perhaps you can go through these basics quickly, but in practice, the majority of training involves perfecting the basics, even with Grand Prix horses.

Structure your daily work as follows:

### 1  *Warm-Up Session*
This part is about warming up the muscles, checking to see if your horse is healthy, and getting him relaxed. During this time, start reviewing his reaction to your aids. Ask yourself: "Does my horse still understand me?" "Are we still speaking the same language?" Go through everything very systematically—every training session. Ask yourself more questions: "Does my horse respond well to a touch from my leg?" "Does he come back immediately when I ask him to do so with my reins?" "Does he relax his jaw from a resisting hand?" Test these responses and ensure that your

*Your horse's "trust" in you, together with his muscular development, is the main indication of whether or not your training program is working well. For this reason, Tineke and Imke observe their horses a great deal during their daily routine. They make sure that the horse's muscles are developing properly, in particular, the muscles on the top of the neck and the hindquarters. They also look for bright eyes and a shiny coat, as well as a horse that shows increasingly more confidence in and friendliness toward his rider. Evidence of these positive signs indicate that the horse is physically and mentally open to you.*

RIDE HORSES WITH AWARENESS AND FEEL

aids are confirmed according to the Question and Answer method. This gives the horse self-confidence. When everything is right, it is time for a little more difficult work.

*2  Work or Performance Session*

The development of the horse's body and mind is the main theme of the work session. You make your horse stronger and more supple by systematically moving his limits. As your horse's rider, you are his sports psychologist, personal trainer, and physical therapist. You can recognize a well-ridden horse by its beautifully developed muscles. This is done by shortening and lengthening bundles of muscle and allowing them sufficient rest in between. We do this in our training.

Improving reactivity is also part of the work. Try to make your horse react to the aids with increasing sharpness. This process sometimes leads to the edge of what Kyra Kyrkland (in the final chapter of this book) calls the "stretch zone" and the "panic zone," in which you come to the limit of his capacity at that moment and must immediately take a step back. Panic causes tension and the flight response. This is wrong. Training to the limit, however, cannot be abandoned—every fitness trainer knows that physical development is only possible through searching for the limits.

However, you are not only your horse's fitness trainer and physical therapist but also his educator—even his psychotherapist. People sometimes forget that the horse's mental development is a primary objective of training, too. Attention to the horse's body and mind are equally important: strive for a healthy mind in a healthy body.

Learning new exercises and perfecting them also belong in the work sessions. Keep in mind the principles from chapter 5 when doing these exercises. Determine the desired Target Behavior and train that Target Behavior according the Question and Answer principles, in other words, Action, Pressure, Reaction, and Reward.

*3  Rest (or Cool Down)*

At this time, you finally give your horse the chance to catch his breath, allow the sweat to evaporate from his coat, and let him relax.

## Deep and Round vs. Classical?

In the past, it was mostly strong men in the military who competed horses; now, we live in an age that sees many more women riders. The average woman may have less muscle power, but makes up for it with more "feel" than the average man! According to Tineke, this might be a reason why many successful women, such as Nicole Uphoff, Margit Otto Crepin, Isabell Werth, and Anky van Grunsven have successfully applied a training method based on a deeper head position during training. Whatever is written and said about this form of training, we believe

**The warm-up is about getting your horse to relax and carefully testing the aids. In the work session, you are your horse's sports psychologist, fitness trainer, and physical therapist. You sometimes seek to find the limits of your horse's mental and physical capabilities of *that* moment but avoid fear and tension. In the rest phase, you let your horse catch his breath and allow the sweat to evaporate.**

that their horses are happy athletes. "Lightness" is a word that comes into our minds as we see their horses perform. It might be interesting to look more into the details of this training method.

If you are not strong, you have to be smart, which, in our opinion, the above-mentioned female riders have been. Smarter than almost any other rider before them. That's why they have won so many big competitions. We might have been a bit critical on some aspects of international dressage judging in this book, but international judges are not blind. It is not just a big mistake that these riders and their horses have dominated international dressage. Also, for the audience, competitive dressage has become much more interesting to watch. We do not believe in the oft-quoted saying, "Everything was so much better in the old days!" Thank goodness, there is evidence on film and in photos that back up this opinion.

Training a powerful "flight" animal to become an even stronger athlete, and to work with you, not against you, is quite a job. It is not only not easy but sometimes dangerous. These riders have brilliantly succeeded in creating wonderful partnerships with their horses. So why are they using a deep-and-round head position in their training?

## The Science behind Riding Deep and Round

Most experienced riders have discovered that they can sit better on a horse that has dropped his head than on one that keeps his head high. What is the reason for this? Let's pay attention to anatomy. In the past, people in the horse world had a different understanding of equine biomechanics. For example, they viewed the horse's back as a structure with little flexibility resting on four "pillars"—the legs. More recently, scientists reviewed this thinking, and started to liken the horse's structure to a suspension bridge, with the horse's back "hanging" on the four pillars instead. The horse's abdominal muscles and the muscles under the longitudinal axis of the spinal column (minor psoas and iliopsoas muscles) keep these "pillars" together and play an essential role in the horse's "core stability." These muscles prevent the back of the horse (the thoracic and lumbar vertebrae) from "dropping." But when the abdominal muscles get weak, for instance, after a broodmare has given birth to several foals, it is not unusual to see a back dropped after a while. The weight of the rider, sitting on the back of his horse, can cause the same effect. A "dropped" back cannot "swing" easily and the back's muscles cannot be developed well from this position.

In 1947, zoologist E. Slijper created the model of the so-called "'archer's bow and string" concept. This model, generally agreed upon in the scientific world, presents the horse's spinal column as a like a bow being held under tension by the string (the abdominal wall and muscles under the spinal column). We use this "bow-and-string" theory quite often, to

*Since 1999, Tineke and Imke have trained regularly with Anky Van Grunsven and Sjef Janssen. "Feel" is the main factor in their training, and Anky's riding skill and success are perfect examples of this. About the couple's training, Tineke says: "Sjef has provided new challenges. Of course, my classical foundation was not suddenly worthless, but I definitely needed to train in a different way—with more 'feel,' more creativity, and more variety. I had to stop 'just' using my legs and think about all the aids that I had always 'just' given. The most important thing I learned was to begin more from my horse's perspective, and because of this, I was able to develop much more 'feel.'"*

explain our training method to our pupils.

Veterinarian Dr. René van Weeren of the University of Utrecht has published data on the influence of the horse's head position on this "bow-and-string" mechanism. The lowering of the head lifts the spine and makes the back arch. According to van Weeren and physiotherapist Solange Schrijer, "the role of the abdominal muscle group is clear, it is one of the mechanisms—always in combination with the sub-lumbar musculature—that draws the bow, and lifts the back. On the other hand, a high head position and lifting of the neck, have the opposite effect: the back is 'stretched' and the vertebral column thus assumes a hollow position."

From experience many good riders already know that a low head is the basis of riding and training. To be sure that a horse is using his back muscles well enough, almost all top trainers make their horses stretch forward and downward at any given moment. Training your horse by alternating a lower head position (lengthening) with a shorter position has a positive influence on the "bow and string" mechanism, and keeps the back flexible. It also causes the hind legs to come more under the body. A research project was conducted in Uppsala, Utrecht, and Zürich (van Weeren, Meyer, Roepstorff, Weishaupt) on the effect of training in the deep-and-round position. It showed clearly that this position can contribute to more elastic movements ("positive range of motion").

Not only does this training method contribute to sport horses getting better results in competition, it also prevents injuries and can cure

*Training Phase 7: "Deep and round": we seldom ride much deeper than Imke is demonstrating here.*

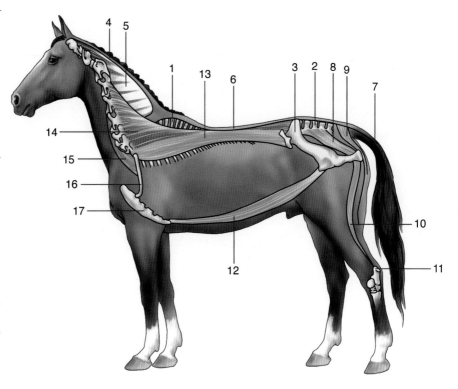

1. Vertebral column with dorsal spinous processes
2. Sacrum
3. External point of hip and hip bone
4. The cord-like connection of the nuchal ligament that forms the top part of the neck
5. The flat portion of the nuchal ligament that connects the wither and chest with the cervical vertebrae
6. The uppermost ligament of the back
7. The uppermost ligament of the tail
8. The elastic ligament that connects the sacrum with the pelvis
9. The uppermost part of the muscle that connects the sacrum with the pelvis and the hock
10. The lowest part of the muscle that connects the pelvis with the hock
11. The uppermost part of the hock and the Achilles tendon
12. The abdominal muscle that connects the pelvis with the sternum
13. The long back muscle
14. The long back muscle divides at the base of the neck
15. The long neck muscle that connects the first rib with the neck (important for lengthening the neck)
16. The first rib
17. The sternum

problems in horses. In human medicine it is well known that physical therapy for back problems involves the strengthening of the back and stomach muscles. Every serious rider should work in the gym to improve his balance and "train" his body through a combination of stretching and lengthening exercises.

The positive effects of stretching on the horse's core stability were recently described by Professor Hilary Clayton and Narelle Stubs in a very interesting practical guide on the positive effects of stretching and mobilization exercises on the horse on the ground. Their book is called *Activate Your Horse's Core* (Sport Horse Publications, 2008).

There is also a positive *psychological* effect of riding with a lower head position experienced by many riders: the horse is more relaxed and able to concentrate better on the rider. Less "force" (meaning strength) is needed to control him. This might be one of the main reasons that so many successful female riders use this training method.

Unfortunately there is not yet much research available on the psychological effect on the horse of riding deep and round. Marianne Sloet van Oldruitenborch-Oosterbaan of the Faculty of Veterinary Medicine at the University of Utrecht drew positive conclusions from her research with veterinary students on the effects of a deep-and-round training position. In Maastricht, a study on stress (heartbeat-interval method) by sports physiologist Eric van Breda showed that top dressage horses that are trained deep and round don't experience any more stress than ordinary riding school horses.

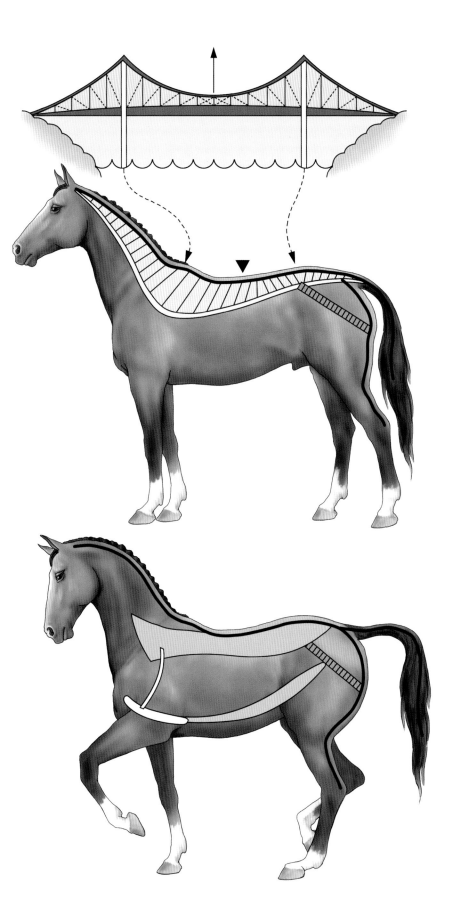

The structure of the horse's back is comparable to a suspension bridge, by which the horse's back "hangs," so to speak, on the four pillars (the legs). The topline of the back is brought upward, by the action of the horse's abdominal muscles and the muscles that lie under the longitudinal axis of the spinal column. These muscles connect the "pillars" together. They prevent the spinal column from "dropping." A dropped back can never swing. The muscle under the spinal column (illopsoas muscle) also causes the pelvis to rotate and the hind legs to come more under the body.

Every experienced rider has discovered that he can sit better on a horse that drops his head than on one that keeps his head high, provided that the hind legs step under the horse's body. If the rider positions the front end deep without keeping the hind legs active, the intended effect will not be achieved.

*Riding "deep and round" also has risks. The horse must be given time to gradually become accustomed to this position. After all, gymnasts do not learn how to do a split in 10 minutes. Furthermore, this method should not lead to just "hand riding." Riding a horse "deep and round" using just the hands, without active hindquarters and complete tempo control, does not work. Furthermore, the horse must feel totally safe in this round position. Important basic principles are "less pressure" and more lightness in the round position, and if pressure must be used, then it should last only a very short time.*

We are not finished with such studies, and that is a good thing in itself. However, we should remember that science cannot answer all our questions. Every training method stands or falls with the right application, which requires a great deal of rider "feel," and "feel" is difficult to express in scientific terms and even more difficult to measure.

Thank goodness classical dressage has given us a good way of checking to see when a horse is truly in self-carriage: when a rider gives away his reins for at least two strides, the horse should remain, on his own, in the same outline (head position) and same tempo. If the horse changes his head position or speed, he is not in self-carriage.

## The Politics behind Riding Deep and Round

The fact that Dutch trainers and scientists are involved in the development and progress of training methods for horses is not a coincidence. Dutch society has always been open to change. Being open to new development is the only way a very small country can be successful. This is exactly what happened in Dutch dressage and breeding. We took the best from the rest of the world and tried to improve it.

We should admit that not everything newly developed is automatically positive. Also mistakes are made in the "process" of change, and there are, unfortunately, examples of bad riding and training in Holland, like in any other country. Excessive use of riding deep and round is bad. But, bad riding is not synonymous with deep-and-round riding.

A negative reaction toward new ideas and initiatives is hardly unusual—resistance to change often comes from countries or groups with strong positions, and is a natural way of defending a consolidated position. Dressage is a very traditional world. New development is often seen as abuse to the "classical traditional roots."

However, it should be noted that the new deep-and-round training was introduced by the German show jumper Alwin Schockemöhle in the 1970s, and successfully transferred to dressage by German dressage riders. The first criticism of it was published in a German magazine reacting to the training methods of double Olympic Champion, Nicole Uphoff of Germany. So, it seems not to be so much a German-Dutch political dressage issue, but more of a discussion between progress and tradition.

The criticism became heated after Dutch rider Anky van Grunsven and her trainer Sjef Janssen were highly successful in international dressage, and openly explained—in clinics and demonstrations—their use of riding deep and round. Further discussion became colored with emotion and based on subjective criteria. It was one of the better FEI decisions to organize a seminar with trainers, researchers, and judges on this matter.

On January 31, 2006, the FEI Veterinary Committee organized a seminar in Lausanne on the use of the deep and round position in the training of show horses. The participants came from different scientific disciplines. The FEI seminar reached the following conclusion:

*"Based on presentations of different research projects in the field of exercise physiology, radiology, biomechanics and schooling, the meeting reached the preliminary conclusion that, when applied by skilled trainers, there was no scientific evidence that this method was abusive to the horse."*

Fortunately a bit more information from more objective researchers entered the discussion. It was perceived that, as in all training methods, the focus should not be on the training method itself but on the way it is brought into practice by riders and trainers. Several scientists, who were present at this seminar, concluded that this method—when applied by skilled riders and trainers—can have advantages from a biomechanical, anatomical, and psychological point of view. Through the research of these scientists the advantages of riding deep and round became more or less scientifically explainable.

Used by unskilled riders and trainers the training method of riding deep will have disadvantages—like every other training method. In 1996, the French authors Denoix and Pailloux, had already described the ad-

vantages and disadvantages of riding deep and round in their book *Physical Therapy and Massage for the Horse* (Trafalgar Square Books, 2001). They expressed clearly that the way of training a horse in a low and short neck position should be restricted, since excessive use—like every unbalanced form of training—can cause injury.

Unfortunately, the negative aspects of this training method, brought to people's attention by unskilled riding or in cases of excessive use, are sometimes used to condemn the method of riding deep and round in general. Selective use of pictures of a bad moment, which every rider-horse combination can have, is used to "prove" that riding deep is abusive to a horse. Top combinations are sometimes shown in a "bad" position, as they can be photographed or filmed at any moment during their warm-ups at competitions where an awkward moment can easily occur. Some journalists and authors used pictures of such "bad" moments of riders riding deep, and selected only "good" moments of traditional riders to publish in their articles or books. This is a rather subjective approach and does not prove anything.

We have experienced difficulties creating an international debate on training methods among trainers and riders, as we have done in Holland. Although the subject seems to be now discussed thoughtfully among judges and scientists, many riders and trainers—the "gurus" of international dressage—seem only to think in "black and white." They either avoid any discussion at all, or take an almost fundamentalistic point of view, without room for reasonable doubt.

We would like any debate to concentrate on the general principles of the training method: on *who* can ride deep and round and *how* one should ride deep and round. In our opinion, any discussion should focus less on the horse's posture but more on the lightness of the rein contact and the horse's self-carriage. This is the message we want to communicate in this book.

RIDE HORSES WITH AWARENESS AND FEEL

The general principle against "rough" riding and any abuse of the horse is, of course, of great importance and one we share in to the utmost. We believe that the best way to protect sport horses is to create openness and honesty. In Holland, the approach to our sport is very open. The Dutch pushed for exercise arenas at the big shows to be open to the public. Riders demonstrate in clinics how they train, and our schooling sessions at our Academy are always able to be watched: all pupils, guests, and clients can attend at every moment. We have demonstrated our way of training in all aspects at hundreds of clinics and workshops. Our Federation has organized meetings for trainers who are both for and against deep riding, and we at the Academy present an annual international seminar, the Global Dressage Forum, to stimulate discussion among all involved in our sport, as we believe that an international exchange of information and debate can only make our sport better. This openness though makes us rather vulnerable to people who use the "war" against modern dressage as a political tool in the sport.

We just do not believe that training has become more "violent" or abusive over the years—it has become more open. There is stewarding at the competitions and cameras all around. We have been in the middle of equestrian sport for the last 40 years and we have seen a lot of good progress. This does not mean that we should avoid self-criticism. Criticism makes one better.

In our clinics and lessons we express clearly that we are very much against excessive use of riding deep and round and we also point out to our pupils that there are risks associated with riding deep when riders or trainers do not adhere to the basic principles of welfare and good horsemanship and use the method incorrectly. You are on the wrong path if you find yourself using enough force to frighten your horse. Of course, this applies to every training system. (Incidentally, we would not be surprised if training with too much force when combined with a high neck position is worse for a horse than using force with a low neck position, if we look well into the facts of recent research.)

As we've said before, the ultimate proof of good training is *lightness* and *self-carriage*.

There are scientific indications that well-balanced use of training with a deep-and-round head position of the horse facilitates elasticity of the movements and reduces stress. However, we must remember that every training method stands or falls with correct application. In our opinion, the debate about training methods should not focus too much on the outline of the horse (head down) but more on the lightness of the rein contact and whether or not he is in self-carriage. We believe that a horse in self-carriage is a "happy athlete."

## Conditions of Riding Deep and Round

The following basic principles are important to consider when training deep and round:

1. The deeper position should be developed over a lengthy period; the horse must be accustomed to it slowly.
2. Do not begin shortening the neck too soon but first ride the horse forward and downward with a long neck.
3. Training deep and round is only possible when you have tempo and

position control, and the horse gives to the bit lightly from a resisting hand.

4  The horse must "let his head fall" of his own accord; pulling him round is counter-productive.

5  The basic principle is "training with less pressure." In the round position, the contact is very light; the weight of the reins is enough. To check to see if the horse is in self-carriage the rider must always be able to give the reins completely away for a stride or so. The horse must then maintain his head position and speed.

6  A horse in the deeper position should give you the feeling that he enjoys the position and feels safer in it.

7  Inexperienced riders should not train too deep.

A rider should "invite" his horse to "let his head fall," and riding deep should be more "leg work" than "hand work." It should always be coupled with relaxation of the topline and the hind legs stepping forward underneath by keeping the horse forward and in front of the rider's leg.

In the show ring, riders usually get low marks when their horse goes *too deep* rather than staying *too high*. We believe this is because a judge can easily spot a horse "behind the vertical," which gives you a lower score. This is unfortunate because we believe that a *relaxed horse slightly behind the vertical in light contact with the rider* is technically much better than a *tense horse with a tight back whose nose is in front of the vertical*. However, the rules do not permit a horse to be "behind the vertical," and every novice judge can see when a horse is in this position. But, a horse that moves with a loose back and no blockages throughout his entire body is more difficult to see.

We hope that the current discussion on "deep and round" adds more emphasis on self-carriage and light contact to the technique of judging horses.

## Using Correctional Devices

In principle, we are not against using auxiliary reins, but using such a device comes with added risks. We use these only as a corrective device, and we always point out the potential downsides to our students. The leverage action of draw reins can cause a rider to use too much pressure. Then, some riders are tempted to start a "power game" of who can pull the hardest. Force always deteriorates into pressure and tension, neither of which go hand in hand with rider "feel." Refining feel is the most important principle in our training method, so use of force and creation of tension have no place at all in the system. Remember that a horse is an animal that fears danger—pressure or tension—and can take flight, accordingly.

We occasionally use draw reins at the Academy as a corrective device, for example, with a young stallion that shows too much bravado. In this case, draw reins are really about the rider's safety. For example, if the stallion threatens to rear, the rider can at least intervene.

With an inexperienced rider who does not have an independent seat and whose horse cannot relax, the use of draw reins creates a vicious circle from which there is no escape. Such a rider needs to improve his seat with lessons on the longe line and the horse in side reins. However, we sometimes recommend using Thiedemann reins. These correct the horse's position when he raises his head too high but stop their rein action the moment the horse drops it. This effect can also be achieved with a standing martingale.

## Conclusion

The FEI and we at the Academy all strive toward the same end result: the horse as a "happy athlete," that is, one that is light, athletically developed, enjoys his work, is nicely on the aids, moves over the back, has impulsion, and is relaxed and in self-carriage.

Your horse determines the training schedule, so you always have to start with his *individual physical and mental characteristics*. Your goal is for him to be physically and mentally "open" to you. A horse that is open is comfortable to ride. To achieve this, we at the Academy train using our total method, which focuses on removing the horse's physical and mental blockages. In addition, we work a great deal on "feel." It is important to work incrementally—step by step. The slowest way is always the fastest way at the end of the day!

Riding deep and round is only a part of our total training system at the Academy. We see it as an addition to the existing classical method of riding. You make the horse's muscles relaxed and looser, suppler, and stronger by varying his position a lot. However, varying his position—alternating between long, short, deep, round, and high—is only possible with tempo control. We try to avoid an extremely deep position of the head.

Force is never allowed; lightness is the basic principle with everything and through it, you loosen the horse's entire body, by which he opens himself to you. A horse that is physically and mentally open lets his muscles become completely relaxed *and* he feels safe with you. If your horse is in self-carriage, you can be his psychologist, fitness trainer, and physical therapist. There is practically no hands-on physical therapy that can loosen a horse's back as well as a good rider can.

A horse that is trained properly according to our system is also easy to ride with his head in front of the vertical; therefore, you can ride him in a more elevated position, and with correct contact. You develop your horse into an athlete by varying this position and his tempo. Riding becomes more comfortable and the horse's movement becomes more beautiful.

There are risks associated with riding deep and round when a rider applies the training position incorrectly. If you use any force to achieve the position, you are on the wrong path. Force always ends up causing tension, and tension and good training do not go together. Auxiliary reins do not belong with the deep-and-round training method, but they may be used exclusively as a corrective tool in the hands of a professional trainer.

Follow the training steps below and note their systematic order:

1 Give a young or new horse the chance to get used to you and to relax.
2 Apply your leg and rein aids separately.
3 Train tempo control: refine the reaction to your leg aids and rein aids.
4 Teach your horse to "give" to the bit from a resisting hand.
5 Develop the game of Question and Answer through tempo changes.
6 Invite your horse to "let his head fall" (first phase of position control).
7 Work on athletic development by shortening and lengthening your horse (second phase of position control).
8 Work on removing all blockages.
9 Allow elevation and collection to happen naturally.
10 Strive for your horse to "open" himself to you physically and mentally, which is demonstrated by a light rein contact and self-carriage.

## Temperamental Horses or Lazy Horses

Due to Anky van Grunsven's many successes with temperamental, "hot" horses, it has been suggested that riding deep and round is mainly suited to this type. Given that this method only works when a horse is in front of the leg, people think that a "hot" horse is an advantage. However, it is almost as difficult to get tempo control with a hot horse by teaching him to go slower without pulling on the reins as it is to make a lazy horse quicker. *Tempo control is the basic principle of this method.*

Hot or lazy, riding deep and round is actually suitable method for all breeds of horses. We now have experience with all kinds. The method also works particularly well when correcting problem horses.

One of Tineke's hobbies is training Friesian stallions. Initially, she rode the breeding stallion Reyert; now she is training Wilke (C van de Wijdewormer). She is pleased to be able to get the very best out of them and ride them to their highest capacity by training them deep and round. Wilke is also being trained according to our Academy Bartels total method.

Your goals must be realistic with your horse's capability in mind. There are not many horses like Salinero. And even though most horses are not capable of the Olympic level there is no reason to dismiss training deep and round. The horse determines *when* you apply it. However, if you do train deep and round, then do it correctly. The same can be said, of course, for all methods of training!

Tineke greatly enjoys training her Friesian stallion Wilke (sire: Fabe 348 x Tjimme, owner: Stal Wijdewormer and Stal Bartels). By training various types and breeds of horses, Tineke has experienced that the training methods, such as described in this book, apply to all horses. However, your goals must always be geared toward the capabilities of your horse. Not every horse is a top athlete suited for the Olympics.

*Tineke has trained many horses to Grand Prix. In this photo, she is riding one of her favorites: the breeding stallion Broere Jazz (sire: Cocktail x Ulster, owner: Stal Bartels).*

# Tineke on Her Daily Training

IN THIS DESCRIPTION, I start with the assumption that my horse already has some training and will not just go off running and bucking. If he does have some excess energy, then he first has to get rid of it on the longe line: I'm not 20 years old anymore! Incidentally, our horses typically do not misbehave. They are usually not too fresh because they come out of their stalls at least two, and preferably, three times a day, and can blow off steam in the pasture or paddock. In hand, they learn disciplined behavior, just like under saddle. They buck in their free time—not when I am sitting on them!

On a normal day, I start with at least 10 minutes of walk, first on a long rein so that the horse can move freely as he wants. I pay attention to whether he starts out stiffer than usual or immediately moves off in a big walk. If I feel stiffness or notice anything abnormal, I immediately watch him move on the longe line in the arena or on hard ground. If his trot is not the same going both left and right, I call the vet. Actually, I do this regularly and have every horse checked several times a year.

After a few minutes of walking, I start taking up the reins a bit and seek a light contact with the mouth. I do not ask for more than a little tempo control with my legs and hands. Then I allow my horse to give to the bit. I slowly try to get him to concentrate on me.

After 10 minutes, we start trotting. This is still the warm-up. I trot loosely and relaxed—but certainly on the bit—and do tempo changes. First, I ask for tempo control and then position control, always in the same order. I try to get the horse to drop his head and follow the contact in the reins. I especially try to avoid his leaning on my hands. However, I do not mind if he is a bit strong in my hands and canters nicely forward at this stage. I prefer to ride with a lighter seat in the canter, sometimes in two-point.

After 15 to 20 minutes, I start doing more transitions. I try to do these with a "forward-downward feel," by which I mean that I want to feel that the horse wants to stretch his neck forward and downward, without pulling on the reins. I do not let him stretch his neck but feel that he could at any moment I wanted.

If I want to ride a transition but feel that the horse is getting blocked, I do not complete the transition. I usually feel when a blockage is coming because the horse comes against my hand or gets behind my leg. Then, I just ride on in the original tempo and try the transition again. I do this until I get a good feeling in the transition.

I try to vary my basic work as much as possible. I keep changing the tempo and now "challenge" my horse. For example, I prepare for a trot-walk transition, but just before the walk, I ride forward again. I try to ask for more by continually doing something other than what he wants to do. When he is too eager to go back to the walk, then I ride him forward. If he would much prefer to keep trotting and is pulling, I give him a stronger half-halt.

Everything is geared toward my aids becoming lighter and smaller. I give an aid just once and allow the horse to do what I ask until I give him a new aid. When he does not react optimally to my aid, I repeat the aid as soon as possible but a bit more strongly. If he responds, I give with my hands. I try to let my horse think forward. He must want to go forward on his own before I do a down transition because I do not use my legs in a downward transition. The "forward" desire in such a transition must come from my horse alone. Combining leg aids and rein aids can lead to confusion.

I am now in the middle of the work session: I must be completely in charge of the tempo and be able to go forward quickly as well as slow down just as fast. My horse has to think with me and maintain the tempo I ask for on his own. A single touch of my legs must be enough to ride forward an entire long side or more, until I ask for a slower tempo with a small half-halt. Sometimes, I use my voice, but I try to only use it consistently. It can be very helpful when your horse knows exactly how he should respond to a certain voice command.

The entire Ten Training Phases are about the principle of communication—seeking harmony and making the aids as small as possible. I continually try to teach my horse to do as much as possible on his own and to carry himself.

I also do a lot of gymnastic exercises in my work sessions by alternating my horse's position between long and short as well as deep and high. This is the core of every training session and my horse should definitely exert himself. I often hear my stallions sigh when I approach their limit. I recognize that feeling from my own experiences at the gym. If you feel that the horse has given his best effort, then a bit of rest at the walk is the best reward. My work time always includes several walk breaks.

Until my horse is five or six years old, I actually seldom do exercises other than transitions, shoulder-in, and turns. With shoulder-in, 75 percent of the work happens in the corner before the exercise. By concentrating on that preparatory piece, you automatically work on preparing for your test.

Every ride is full of surprises, so I try to not to have a "standard program." I pay attention to the effect of my work on the horse. And that effect determines everything. I want tempo control; I want my horse to drop his head, letting go forward and downward; and I want control over his position. A horse that is five or six should be able to go from moving with his nose over the ground to moving upright in front of the vertical within just a few strides from a touch of my legs.

The most important work is actually playing with the tempo and then playing with the position. In addition, I naturally pay close attention to my own position, which happens at our place automatically because when you train together, you pay attention to one another. We give each other pointers everyday: sit more quietly; soften your hand; keep your legs quiet and do not grip.

Exercises are certainly important when they have major gymnastic value, like shoulder-in and half-steps, starting at age six or seven. I have seen many horses improve greatly through half-steps. Such exercises are always done for a very short period, as their gymnastic value is usually obtained by riding into or out of the exercise. Variety is a most important principle. The horse tells you how to do this—you always do something other than what he wants to do. When he does shoulder-in for 10 meters, ask for something different: faster, slower, more angle. When a horse likes to keep his head and neck high, ask him to go extra "round" and vice versa.

I also think it is important that you sometimes allow things to go wrong. You look for the limits in the work session, and this can only happen if you occasionally exceed them. For example, your horse breaks into the canter from an extended trot. Never punish him for this because, in principle, he did what you asked: "Go forward." Therefore, do not react. Do not reward him, but quietly transition to the trot and try again. The addition of variety and doing the unexpected keeps your horse fresh and attentive. When you always do the same thing, the fun goes away. During show season, also pay attention to the correct show position in the work phase, that is, with the nose just in front of the vertical. If your tempo control is good, you can at regular intervals make the neck position a bit more upright by opening your hands a little and applying your legs to raise the horse's nose. The neck arch should remain round.

The duration of work depends entirely on my horse's age, level of training, and disposition. Fifteen minutes is sometimes long enough for a young horse, let's say age four or five, but I have also spent more than an hour riding a recalcitrant six-year-old. We leave plenty of time for rest and walk our horses out under saddle for at least 10 minutes and then often walk them in hand after that. It is nice for them to be able to walk outside the arena to watch other things going on. In this respect, too, a change in surroundings is very important.

Adding new and different work and changing it up makes our Academy training method fun. You can see our horses "blossom" in the course of their training; they become more beautiful, stronger, healthier, and more "open." They become more tuned into people. This is not a theoretical assertion but a reality that most of our students can confirm. Our training sessions are never private—students are present. I think the biggest myth about riding deep and round is the inference that it constitutes animal abuse and this causes a great deal of misunderstanding. I also find the implication very unfortunate, all the more so because it has been put forth by some people who have not bothered to study the riding-deep method in depth.

Of course, as we've said, incorrect application of the riding-deep method does not contribute to a horse's welfare, but this applies just as much to other ways of riding. If you use this method correctly—the way we've described, I am certain your horse will benefit. And if a method is not used correctly, then the question is, what is worse for the horse? Riding deep badly or riding high badly?

CHAPTER 7

# What We Have Learned from Other Trainers

Global
Dressage
Forum

## The Global Dressage Forums of 2001–2005

In 2000, we came up with the idea of organizing an annual world conference on dressage at the Academy in Hooge Mierde. In the past, the Chair of the International Dressage Trainers Club, Herman Duckeck of Denmark, had organized a trainers' conference every two years, but these were discontinued after his passing.

The Academy wanted to fill this vacuum and took the initiative to organize an annual conference that not only was geared toward trainers but also aimed at encouraging more internal communication throughout the entire sport of dressage. In close consultation with trainers Sjef Janssen, Johann Hinnemann, David Hunt, dressage rider Richard Davison, and dressage judge Mariëtte Withages, a program was put together at the end of 2000, which included the world's best trainers. They came to give clinics and discuss their methods. In addition, equine scientists were invited to talk about their discoveries.

The first Global Dressage Forum was held in September 2001. It immediately drew a great deal of interest. The Forum provided a wonderful opportunity for Academy employees to meet the best trainers in the world. Many of the trainers stayed at the Academy during the Forum and held discussions late into the night about their experiences, basic principles, innovations, and problems. The Global Dressage Forum became an important source of inspiration for the Academy and its visitors. For this reason, we have included short summaries of several clinics in this book. The summaries are from the official reports drafted by Bernadette Faurie and Jane Kidd.

*Jürgen Koschel, 2001*

## Global Dressage Forum 2001

### TRAINER: Jürgen Koschel
### TOPIC: "Sympathetic Control": Training In Hand

Jürgen Koschel gave an interesting clinic at the first Global Dressage Forum. Koschel is an experienced Grand Prix rider and trainer, who has served as Chef d' Equipe for several countries, including the Netherlands (1996–2000). He introduced work in hand as an historical system that is frequently used in the classical riding schools of Vienna, Saumur, and Jerez. Koschel's guide is always the German Training Scale: rhythm and regularity, suppleness and relaxation, contact, impulsion, straightness, and collection. This is the framework in which all German trainers test their work.

In-hand training is mainly used to accustom the horse to the trainer and strengthen its muscles without having to bear the weight of the rider on its back. This type of training, frequently used at the Spanish Riding School, is something for those with specialized knowledge and is not entirely risk-free. Therefore, Koschel emphasized safety several times. The fact is that the trainer is very vulnerable in his position behind the horse if he does not take good precautionary measures and pay constant attention to safety.

In this in-hand training method, the whip is an extension of the trainer's arm and not an instrument for punishment. An important objective is for the horse to learn to accept the whip with confidence. The four touch points on the horse are: the fetlock, the hock, the tendon above the hock, and the croup. With the horse in side reins and driven from behind with the whip, the trainer asks for half-steps (*halbe Tritte*). These are comparable to "dribbles" (shortened steps) forward. They are used to introduce piaffe but are intended as a gymnastic exercise at this stage.

Koschel usually trains his horses in hand quite deep and round, and concentrates on developing trust, impulsion, and what he calls "sympathetic control."

### What We Learned
*We were impressed by this trainer's calm and clear manner; however, we seldom use in-hand training and certainly not with young horses because we have not mastered this type of work.*

### TRAINER: Sjef Janssen
### TOPIC: Quickening Responses

In this historic clinic—Bonfire's last appearance at this level—Sjef Janssen and Anky van Grunsven presented their Olympic champion to their fellow trainers in a unique training session. Sjef described his career as a self-made man and introduced physical therapist Solange Schrijer, who gave a comprehensive presentation on the effects of training deep and round on the muscular system. The objective of this training method is to create a balance between the back muscles and the abdominal muscles. According to Schrijer, these muscles can only be developed optimally from a round starting position.

Anky demonstrated this theory with Bonfire. A quiet warm-up with lots of lengthening and shortening was followed by a work phase with a lower neck position. Sharpening responses is the most important part of the work phase. The rider plays with the responses according to the aid-reaction-relaxation principle. Janssen asserted that the canter is the best gait for developing the abdominal muscles.

"Playing with variety" is important not only for a horse's physical development but also very important for his mental development. Anky and Bonfire demonstrated a great deal of variety in every exercise. Given that the training process is so diversified, it is important to have guidance from an experienced instructor. Not every rider should just go experiment with this method without supervision. The horse always tells you what you should do and how far you can go. "You have to learn how to read the horse," says Janssen.

### What We Learned
*We will remember this clinic for some time to come. It was the first time we heard such a clear explanation of the anatomical effect of training deep and round. In addition, we were impressed by the variety in each exercise and the attention to detail.*

### TRAINER: Kyra Kyrklund
### TOPIC: Comfort Zone and Panic Zone

Rider Kyra Kyrklund, originally from Finland, has lived in Flyinge, Sweden, for a long time. Imke worked for Kyra in Flyinge for almost a year. Kyra always starts with the rider's position and seat. These have to be correct before you can influence the horse. Only a rider who can sit balanced can create a balanced horse.

Kyra used various interesting examples to show how horse and rider affect one another. For example, she stood in front of the horse, facing toward his head. She then took hold of the reins near the bit and pulled on them. Her objective was to let the rider feel how much contact was required for a *resisting* hand and how much to soften the contact immediately after the horse responds to the resistance; in other words, when the horse gives to the bit, it is immediately rewarded by a *giving* hand.

Kyra uses an interesting expression for the term half-halt: "trash bin." She thinks it is the term into which we try to put everything that we do not understand. According to Kyra, the concept of the half-halt needs to

*Sjef Janssen, 2001*

*Kyra Kyrklund, 2001*

be better researched and thus better explained.

Young riders need to learn to sit properly and communicate clearly with their horse. Their reactions should be automatic, in other words, demonstrate *unconscious-competence* (p. 41). Kyra's training starts with the traits of her horses. She explained that she has learned that horses have a "comfort zone," a "stretch zone," and a "panic zone." The rider himself should always stay in the comfort zone—calm and controlled, while playing with the horse's zones and sometimes looking for his limits. Sometimes you can even reach the horse's panic zone, where he becomes afraid, and you must take a step back. Do not be afraid to make mistakes; you can learn from them.

Kyra is one of the few dressage trainers who pays a lot of attention to various animal training systems. She explained that her development included observing others a great deal, such as the classic Russian and Western trainers and even circus people, dolphin trainers, and dog trainers doing clicker training. These observations have made her aware of the effects of primary and secondary rewards as well as teaching by combining impressions, that is, *association*.

**What We Learned**
*We consider Kyra Kyrklund the "professor" among trainers. She thinks about everything in an original, intellectual, and creative way. She has taught us to "look outside." She immerses herself in the psychology of the horse. We find her an unusually inspiring person.*

**Global Dressage Forum 2002**

**TRAINER: Robert Dover**
**TOPIC: A Half-Halt Is the Collection of Forward Energy**

Robert Dover has competed in six Olympic Games and is a trainer based on the East Coast in the U.S. During his clinic at the second Global Dressage Forum in October 2002, he mainly focused on the "new countries" in the dressage world: "Be realistic, get the best trainers, buy the best horses, and let your riders show where the best riders are, that is, Germany." His clinic included an explanation of his training formula, which according to him, is geared to all kinds and types of horses. The warm-up for every horse, regardless of age, begins with stretching: the elastic lengthening and shortening of the neck in a downward line. The horse's body should be made round. This exercise should be alternated with periods of trot and walk on a long rein in order to loosen the muscles.

Next, the "gymnastic work" begins, what Dover also calls the "rubber band method." The basic principle of this method is that the horse can be made long and short without losing his rhythm. Further, he does half-

*Robert Dover, 2002*

halts, which he describes as "the collection of forward energy." A half-halt is not quite stopping and then riding forward again. The most important thing is that the horse, even in collection, always maintains a feeling of extension, building up a kind of "reserve energy," so to speak.

After stretching and gymnastic work, come the exercises. These are done in the position that the rider asks of the horse. All head positions—high and low—must be possible. Dover cites Anky van Grunsven as a perfect example of this because she can ride her horses in exactly the position she wants ("perfect adjustability"), and she keeps her horses happy in their work.

In the last phase of training, Dover cools down the horse the exact same way he started: by alternating stretching with periods of walk and trot on a long rein.

### What We Learned
*Dover's principle of riding is "perfect adjustability;" that is, the ability to ride a horse in every tempo and every position the rider desires. We like this. If a horse can go "deep and round," but the rider cannot immediately bring his neck position back up again at any moment he wants, then something is not right.*

### TRAINER: Johann Hinnemann
### TOPIC: The Progression of Training

Johann Hinnemann earned his spurs as a rider (team gold and individual bronze at the 1986 World Championships in Toronto) and as a trainer, with students including Coby and Marlies van Baalen. He gave very popular clinics at the Global Dressage Forum in both 2001 and 2002.

*Johann Hinnemann, 2002*

Hinnemann believes that a rider or trainer should have a long-term plan in mind for every horse. Furthermore, he always starts with the German Training Scale: rhythm and regularity, suppleness and relaxation, contact, impulsion, straightness, and collection. The most important characteristics of a good rider are sufficient basic knowledge, patience, and a good, independent seat.

There is only a thin line dividing the exercises a horse knows and those he has yet to learn. First, exercises must always aim to make a horse soft in the bridle and forward. When a problem arises, the horse should be ridden forward and "new energy collected." Hinnemann always begins a training session by riding the horse forward and downward. He does not use this position much in the later work because he believes that the rider should always keep in mind the position required of the horse in tests.

He acknowledged that Anky van Grunsven is very successful with her method and that "many roads lead to Rome"; however, as a trainer, he feels responsible for riders who try to imitate such an example but cannot do it well.

*Ulla Salzgeber, 2003*

**What We Learned**
*This is a classic trainer with a very distinct and identifiable theme in his clinics. The basic principles are solid, the long-term planning is clear, and the approach is always systematic.*

**Global Dressage Forum 2003**

**TRAINER: Ulla Salzgeber**
**TOPIC: The Rider's Seat and the Horse's Enjoyment**

Ulla Salzgeber won the 2001 and 2003 European Dressage Championships and several medals at the Sydney and Athens Olympics. She says the two most important points of her training are:

1 The rider's correct, independent seat
2 The enjoyment the rider and horse get from their work

She thanks Herbert Rehbein and General Stecken for her perfect seat and still focuses on maintaining it everyday. You have to know the human body very well, according to Salzgeber, whose husband is a physical therapist. The principle of the correct seat is the ability of the rider to receive the horse's movement, and to bring his weight on the thigh bones, and let the pelvis and lumbar area swing.

The objective of her training is the gymnastic development of the horse. For this reason, Salzgeber rides her horses in all positions: round, deep, short, long, bent left, and bent right. She begins her warm-up in the walk and rising trot and then checks to see if her horse is responding well to the leg and rein aids. She does small half-halts and directs her work mainly at creating a light connection with the horse's mouth. Every horse needs to learn to move on his own without support from the rider.

Then, she rides the horse rounder and deeper, but she is very careful doing this with young horses. You should never make a horse round using force. A horse must first develop muscles. He must be "nice" in the contact, and he should playfully chew the reins forward out of your hands, when you give them to him.

After the warm-up, Salzgeber usually does gymnastic exercises for a half hour, such as long-short, bending and positioning on curved lines, transitions, and tempo changes. In between, she always lets her horses stretch their neck as a reward and allows them to rest. Everything is aimed at developing the horse's ability to carry himself (self-carriage). For this purpose, she often uses shoulder-in and then plays with the inside leg and outside rein. She almost never uses a whip. "You don't use one in a test," says Salzgeber.

Collection, piaffe, and passage develop from doing transitions: "Transitions, transitions, transitions all the time." Transitions, like tempo changes or changes of gait, are the most important part of Salzgeber's training. In addition, she focuses a great deal of attention on the rider's total control over the tempo. She says, "You can only have position control when you have tempo control."

### What We Learned
*We feel that this clinic falls into the same category as that of Anky and Bonfire—unforgettable. Almost no one can give such an impressive demonstration of the ideal seat as Ulla Salzgeber can. We know few competition dressage riders who can ride a horse better and more effectively. Her statement that position control starts with tempo control is an essential basic fact.*

### TRAINER: Arthur Kottas
### TOPIC: The Tradition of the Spanish Riding School and the Rider's Seat

Arthur Kottas was one of the most important *Oberbereiters* at the Spanish Riding School in Vienna for many years. He believes the goal of classical horsemanship is harmony between rider and horse.

The young riders at the Spanish Riding School spend two to three years being trained on the longe line, without stirrups, as the seat is an essential necessity for correct riding. "The seat is the key to everything," according to Kottas.

Our basic principles are as follows:
- Your horse is your partner.
- Do not repeat exercises too often.
- Do not tire your horse.
- Keep the work simple.
- Pay special attention to hand-leg coordination.
- Seat and leg aids should never be so strong that harmony is lost.

*Arthur Kottas, 2003*

Kottas trains his horses in hand a lot (also see Koschel, p. 136), and this allows them to learn how to bring their weight onto their hindquarters without interference from the rider. Horses are trained in a longeing cavesson, and the aids are given with the whip. Body language is very important in this work.

Important points for working in hand include:
- Make sure that the horse is completely unafraid of the whip.
- Locate the most important touch points for the whip.
- Ensure that the horse's body position is correct (not too short or too deep).
- Make sure that he keeps going forward.
- Halt means immobility.
- The halt must be square and with the hind legs under the body.
- Moving forward must start with the hind legs.

- Teach your horse half-halts with the cavesson.
- Never work with a tense horse.

For work under saddle, it is important to know that there are many different ways of warming up and training. Do not always do exactly the same thing; keep it varied. Ride outside the arena occasionally.

**What We Learned**
*Kottas' correct seat is a textbook example for every rider. The calm he radiates is certainly an enviable quality. Everything about this classical rider and trainer is controlled and disciplined.*

**TRAINER: Holger Schmezer**
**TOPIC: The German System Is Based on the Training Scale**

Holger Schmezer is the German Chef d'quipe. He and Christoph Hess, the Director of Training at the FN, and several young trainers came to Hooge Mierde to discuss the German training system. The German system is outlined in detail in *Richtlinien für Reiten und Fahren*, the dressage bible of every German trainer. The *Ausbildungsskala*, the Training Scale, is at the center of the system:

*Holger Schmezer, 2003*

- Rhythm and regularity
- Suppleness and relaxation
- Contact
- Impulsion
- Straightness
- Collection

- Habituation and familiarization phase
- Development of horizontal balance
- Development of carrying power

- Durchlässigkeit

The practical application of the system was demonstrated by several riders and horses in different age groups. With the youngest group, attention is mainly focused on the horse's natural balance and the ability to lengthen the neck. Suppleness and relaxation is the most important principle in this phase. It is the foundation on which the Training Scale is based. The first building block of that scale, *takt* (rhythm and regularity), can only happen from a foundation of relaxation.

The desire for spectacular movement, as horses are frequently asked to display at auctions, was made a very important point. This *Auktionsreiten* (auction riding) has some rather negative effects, according to veterinarian Gerd Heuschman, who provided commentary on the clinic. A slow, step-by-step approach is much more effective. It gives better results and the horse lasts longer.

Even in later training, the first building blocks of the Training Scale—

such as rhythm, relaxation, and contact—are very important. In every stage, the rider continues working mainly on the basics. Developing the later building blocks—impulsion, straightness, and collection—always requires the first three blocks of the scale to be checked and repeated. They are the foundation for everything.

## What We Learned
*This is what you expect of German experts: a systematic approach. Drawing on his practical knowledge as Chef d'Equipe, Schmezer conveyed his vast experience in a cordial and calm manner, allowing room for the opinions of others.*

## Global Dressage Forum 2004

**TRAINER: Ulrich Kasselmann**
**TOPIC: The Young Horse Deserves Variety**

*Ulrich Kasselmann, 2004*

Ulrich Kasselmann is the biggest buyer and seller of dressage horses in the world. Each year, dozens of horses are trained at his facility. He brought several young auction horses to the fourth Global Dressage Forum.

According to Kasselmann, the most important qualities in a three-year-old horse are relaxation and a good, "pleasantly chewing" mouth. A horse must trust the rider completely before relaxation and submission to the bit can be developed. A young horse should "ask" the rider's hands to go forward and downward and should learn to move in balance with a quietly swinging tail. He should trust the people who work with him and concentrate on his rider.

At Stal Kasselmann, horses are longed before they are ridden. Once started under saddle, they are trained on the double longe twice a week in 15 to 20 minute sessions to improve contact. Young horses are usually not ridden more than three times a week. Stal Kasselmann usually does not train horses with side reins because it is felt these can be too "strong" and therefore act negatively upon the tongue and mouth.

Kasselmann also trains his young dressage horses over small jumps. The three-year-olds and four-year-olds are frequently ridden outside on a galloping track to build up their muscles and strengthen their hind legs.

## What We Learned
*We like the varied training program for young horses. We also think that training over cavalletti or small jumps can be very beneficial. Since then, the Academy has put in its own galloping track, which we use quite often.*

*Jan Brink, 2004*

## TRAINER: Jan Brink
## TOPIC: Control over Length and Rhythm

Swedish dressage rider Jan Brink brought along his top horse Briar and his trainer Kyra Kyrklund for his clinic. The keynote of his training is the rider's ability to be able to relax the horse under all circumstances. If the rider cannot accomplish this at home, then he certainly cannot do it at shows. As soon as the rider gets control over the length and rhythm of his horse's strides, he can get control over the horse's entire body. Then, control over the horse's mind follows.

Brink first let Briar stretch his neck forward and downward, making sure that Briar continued to carry himself. Then, he started doing transitions and tempo changes in the canter. He played with the length of the canter stride on a circle. Strides should get smaller and bigger without the tempo changing. He asked for shorter strides in the trot without going faster or slower, while Briar maintained a relatively long neck.

Although the rider plays with the length and rhythm of the strides, he must always be mindful that he stays sitting straight on top of the horse.

Brink also had a tip for the trainers present: learn to teach clearly. Students do not know if "use leg" or "go forward" means go faster or lengthen the stride. The meaning of such instruction needs to be defined in advance.

Trainers should also teach their students to play with the length of the horse's body. A horse should never hang on the bit, as doing so prevents the hind legs from developing strength. Brink frequently gave the rein and patted Briar on the neck at the same time. The rider should immediately praise the horse for a good response (the same principle as used with clicker training). Moreover, a pat on the neck momentarily "relaxes" the rider's seat. The motion of the hand toward the horse's neck allows the rider to come "off" his seat, and relax. It was very important for Briar to learn to transition to a relaxed walk immediately from every exercise and go directly forward and downward into the hand. Initially, his walk was very tense, and this was the only method that improved it.

Brink also gave some tips for improving the more difficult movements. The passage can be affected by doing changes of rhythm and stride length. The piaffe is often improved by lightening the seat (forward) and positioning the neck a bit deeper. Then the rider plays with the rhythm of the piaffe strides. Pirouette problems can sometimes be helped by doing transitions from the piaffe to the canter, in which the rider must maintain the collection of the piaffe in the canter.

In general, the rider ensures that training sessions offer a continuous variation of tempo and position, effort and rest, and request and reward. Balance is the core concept for horse *and* rider.

**What We Learned**

*Jan Brink is very successful with stallions. Working with them is a unique skill, as we have found out in our career. They require a tactful approach. The tendency of many riders to deal with stallions firmly can work against them. Stallions resist pressure and think it is very macho to occasionally fight back. Although Jan is tall and strong, he rarely uses force. He works with lots of looseness and relaxation, which he can go back to any time he wants. He also keeps his training markedly varied.*

TRAINER: Rudolf Zeilinger
TOPIC: Suppleness Is Never Possible under Pressure

Rudolf Zeilinger is a very successful rider and the Chef d'Equipe of the Danish team. Therefore, his clinic included a training demonstration with Andreas Helgstrand and the well-known Danish stallion Don Schufro. Zeilinger explained that his goal is to connect classical horsemanship with the recently introduced concept of the "happy athlete." The basic principle of both philosophies is a "happy rider," who is relaxed and always in balance both physically and mentally, who sits centered on his horse with an independent seat, and who makes his horse feel safe.

*Rudolf Zeilinger, 2004*

Many young riders these days do not realize how much pressure they are under from parents and trainers. This pressure carries over into their riding, and a horse under pressure can never show suppleness. It is the job of trainers to make clear to parents, owners, and riders that force is useless and that every horse has his limits.

Zeilinger prefers to train his horses in the classical position, with the nose in front of the vertical. He generally trains them more upright than many other top riders, but the neck position in training also depends greatly on the individual horse. The ideal neck position is sought in every exercise, as long as the back stays loose and the hind legs keep coming through. Zeilinger plays with the length of the neck, and the connection between the hand and the horse's mouth is very light. Everything is aimed at preserving and developing the basic gaits, according to Zeilinger. Every horse should be evaluated individually; he will indicate the tempo and rhythm you should ask for in training.

Zeilinger starts training horses early, at age three or four, but the training is playful in the beginning. Horses need three to four years to become strong, find their balance, and build up enough trust in the rider so that they can begin learning the more difficult movements, such as piaffe and passage.

It is a big job to keep your horse happy in all stages of training. For this reason, you should be mindful that any discipline necessary does not come at the expense of mental "ups and downs." We need to ask ourselves each day how much we can do in our training without our horse standing in his stall sour and unhappy at night. Every horse enjoys working hard, so you can put pressure on them. A person is also satisfied after a day of hard work. However, your horse only enjoys hard work when he understands exactly what you ask of him and this only happens if you are consistent and clear.

## What We Learned
*A basic requirement for training a horse to be a happy athlete is a happy rider, who can give his horse a feeling of safety, according to Zeilinger. We think this is a very strong basic principle and one that has stayed with us. Although Zeilinger is not interested in riding deep and round, we still consider him a rider and trainer whose philosophy is not far from ours. He works with the same basic principles as we do, which is to say that the contact should be as light as possible and suppleness cannot be developed under pressure.*

## Global Dressage Forum 2005

**TRAINER: Georg Theodorescu**
**TOPIC: Forward, Straightness, and Regularity**

After a career of 50 years, Georg Theodorescu has become a legend in the dressage world. For his clinic, he brought along his daughter Monica, winner of multiple Olympic medals and World Cup finals. Theodorescu said: "I don't talk much during training sessions; Monica usually only needs one word from me." Indeed, he talked little during his clinic.

The work pace is very slow. Training is built up logically to give the rider the opportunity to bring the horse in balance step by step. This process takes years. Much attention should be given to a correct seat—not just position but also movement of the lower body—as the biggest problems are due to the rider, who keeps bringing the horse out of balance.

Monica began the clinic with the walk, after which she transitioned to rising trot and paid a great deal of attention to forward impulsion, straightness, and regularity. She rode a lot of corners and circles to bring the horse's hindquarters under his body without having to use pressure. In the canter, she did lots of counter-canter with an emphasis on maintaining rhythm, keeping the neck position (nose just in front of the vertical), and keeping the same feel in both reins (straightness).

The horse must be made more supple and stronger. The half-halt, shoulder-in, and half-pass are used for this purpose. The obvious problem that Monica's horse had in the walk (a lateral tendency) made collecting the walk difficult, as collection did not improve this horse's walk. She rode shoulder-in in the walk on a square and did half-steps, which are also used to develop piaffe.

*Georg Theodorescu, 2005*

Theodorescu is not a proponent of the deep-and-round neck position "because it's unnatural when a horse can't look at you as he's standing in front of you."

Theodorescu explained that he definitely does not repeat all the movements regularly. For example, he did not do any flying changes for two months with this demonstration horse. He focuses on one new exercise per week at most and concentrates on another exercise the following week. He alternates intensive training days with easy ones.

### What We Learned
*The calm manner of the rider and trainer were visibly translated into relaxation and trust on the part of the horse.*

### TRAINER: Klaus Balkenhol
### TOPIC: Maintain Natural Talent through Sympathetic Gymnastics

*Klaus Balkenhol, 2005*

As a police officer, Klaus Balkenhol worked his way up with his police horse Rabauke to become a successful member of the German national dressage team. He is now the Chef d' Equipe of the United States and a definite opponent of riding deep and round. He thinks this position is unnatural and demeaning to the horse. Furthermore, it is not classical and therefore does not meet the standard outlined in the German Training Scale.

Balkenhol works according to the German Training Scale. The basic principle of his clinic was as follows: maintain the horse's natural talent in training through sympathetic gymnastic development of the horse's entire body. Balkenhol was assisted in his clinic by Grand Prix rider George Williams, Volker Brommann, and several breeders and riders, who presented mainly young horses.

Training begins from the time a horse is a foal. Horse and man have to get used to one another and develop a bond of trust. Work under saddle begins when the horse is sufficiently strong (mature enough). Once under saddle, the horse must learn half-halts as soon as possible; however, a young horse should not be treated like a dressage horse too soon. Training should stay fun with a lot of variety, and focus on relaxation, suppleness, rhythm, and balance. In that respect, horses are trained much too fast nowadays. Young horses have to perform too soon.

On the subject of tack, Balkenhol recommends checking a young horse's bridle and bit regularly and adjusting these, if required; and choosing a wider, thinner, or thicker bit, as needed. After all, a horse's head and mouth change as he grows. Balkenhol does not recommend using a foregirth, as they are restrictive and can be painful and irritating.

Contact between hand and mouth is essential at every stage of training. This affects movement. There should no longer be resistance in the "center of movement," the mid-section of the horse, and every horse should be able to lower his neck forward and downward.

When a horse is mature, approximately at age five, the experienced rider can slowly start collection. The horse is ridden from back to front into the hand. The horse must learn to always seek contact with the rider's hand. Results of the first phase of training should be as follows:

- Rhythm
- Forward impulsion to the hand
- Good contact between hand and mouth

If these points are in order, then the rider can proceed further with training. He can collect the horse by shortening and lengthening him and teaching him exercises. The rider must ensure that the horse always stays forward and the work is sufficiently varied.

**What We Learned**
*Klaus Balkenhol warned about the negative effects that all the tests have on young stallions—the same is true regarding the championships for young horses. We completely agree with him on these points.*

# Conclusion

Dressage is in a turbulent period of growth, development, and discussion. Its popularity is greater than ever. Riders and horses are better than they were several years ago. Training methods are changing. Dressage shows no longer take place at out-of-the-way facilities; instead, they draw mass attention. The new audience includes fewer "horse people" and more "people with horses," horse lovers who did not grow up with them but who now want to learn as much as possible about them. These people often view horses differently from those who have had horses in their lives forever. One consequence of this change is that more understanding of equestrian sport is needed, and in this book, we have attempted to provide this in a contemporary way. Our explanation is based on practice as much as possible and on our experiences at championships and the Olympics, as well as more than 30 years of giving lessons to hundreds of riders during our lesson and training clinics.

The welfare of the horse is being viewed more critically at the top of the sport than was the case years ago. This sometimes leads to thinking that "everything was better in the old days." We have been involved in the sport long enough to know that this is nonsense. On the contrary, developments over the past 20 years have had many positive effects on the horse. Dressage, once the bastion of physically strong men in the military, has developed into a sport in which the majority of those who practice it are women. The direct result of this is more "feel" and less force in training and riding at the top. But, of course, all that glitters is not gold. Riding nowadays is not always done sensibly and well. With the advent of warm-up arenas open to public viewing, every outgrowth of dressage comes under the magnifying glass. There is nothing wrong with this because it facilitates debate. And discussion is necessary for progress.

We hope that with this book we too can contribute to the discussion and further developments in dressage. With the introduction of the term "happy athlete" into the FEI's rules, dressage has emerged from the somewhat solemn sphere of "horsemanship." Dressage is no longer a mysterious art form but a modern sport. "Happy" stands for welfare; "athlete" stands for physical and psychological development. Just like all other modern sports, dressage is evolving. This evolution is only possible through use of new insights, and new insights bring about change. These changes should be based on respect for history. We hope this book contributes to this.

*Tineke, Imke, and Joep Bartels*

## Bibliography and Web Sites

Bartels, Tineke, *Basisboek Dressuur*, Forte Uitgevers, Utrecht: 2000.

Baumert, Beth, "Collection Just Happens," *Dressage Today*, March 2002.

Burton, D, *The Jekyll/Hyde Nature of Goals: Reconceptualizing Goal Setting in Sport*, 1992

Clayton, Hillary M, *Conditioning Sport Horses*, Sport Horse Publications, 1991.

Cornelis, L. *Typegids MBTI®*, Gorinchem, 2001.

Dierendonck, Machteld van, *The importance of social relationships in horses*, (dissertation), Utrecht University 2006.

Dietze, Susanne von, *Balance in Movement: The Seat of the Rider*, Trafalgar Square Books, North Pomfret, Vermont: 2002.

Eberspächer, H, *Mentale Trainingsformen in der Praxis*, Sportinform, Oberhaching: 1990.

Fédération Equestre International, *The Use of Overbending ("Rollkur") in FEI Competition*, Report of the FEI Veterinary Committee meeting at the Olympic Museum in Lausanne, January 2006.

Gladwell, Malcolm, *Blink*, Penguin: 2005.

Haan, Karin de, "Geen Confectie maar Maatwerk," *De Hoeflslag*, Issue 49, December 2005.

Horn, TS (Ed.), *Advances in Sport Psychology*, pp. 267–297, Human Kinetics, Champaign.

Loon, Ernest van, *Ruiters en rechters deel 2*, AOC de Groene Welle: 2002.

McLean, Andrew, *De waarheid over paarden*, Fontaine: 2005.

Mihaly, Csikszentmihalyi, *Finding Flow*, Harper Collins: 1997.

Mihaly, Csikszentmihalyi, *De weg naar Flow*, Uitgeverij Boom: 1999.

Nideffer, RM, "Concentration and Attention Control Training," In: Williams, J.M. (Ed.), *Applied Sports Psychology*, pp. 257–269, Mayfield: 1986.

*Paardrijden, basisopleiding voor ruiter en paard*, Forte Uitgevers, Utrecht: 2004.

Pochhammer, Gaby, "Zur Entfaltung kommen—statt zur Brust genommen," *Sankt George*, Issue 4, 2003.

Prakke, Hans, *De Kneetstory*, Agiel: 2005.

Roediger, Herman, and Capaldi, Polivy, *Psychologie*, Marc. Academia Press: 1998.

Schirm, R.W., Schoemen, J., *Evolution of Personality*, Baar, Switzerland: 2003.

Schrijer, Solange, and Weeren, René van, "Auf dem falschen Rücken ausgetragen," *Reiterrevue*, Issue 7, 2003.

Schuijers, Rico, *Mentale training in de sport*, Elsevier, Maarssen: 2004.

Sloet van Oldruitenborgh-Oosterbaan, M.M., and Blok, Begeman, Kamphuis, Lameris, Spierenburg, Lashley, "Workload and Stress in Horses: Comparison in Horses Ridden Deep and Round (Rollkur) with a Draw Rein and Horses Ridden in a Natural Frame with Only a Light Rein Contact," *Tijdschrift Diergeneesunde*, Part 131, Issue 5, March 1, 2006.

Visser, Kathalijne, *Horsonality*, E.K. Visser, Heerenveen: 2002.

Voest, Emiel, *Freestyle Training Phase 1 and 2*, www.emielvoest.nl.

Wanless, Mary, *Ride with Your Mind*, Trafalgar Square Books, North Pomfret, Vermont: 1999.

Weeren, René van, and Schrijer, Solange, "Auf dem falschen Rücken ausgetragen," *Reiterrevue*, Issue 7, 2003.

Weis, Richard, www.richardweis.com.

## Thank You!

A number of people and institutions were a part of creating this book, and we owe thanks for the support, information, and inspiration they provided. Here are some of them in alphabetical order:

Boelaarts, Ed (illustrations)

Bronkhorst, Arnd (photos)

Caremans, Dirk (photos)

Dierendonck, van Machteld (adviser, chapter 5)

Fédération Equestre International (Dressage Committee discussions and Rollkur seminar)

Global Dressage Forum (all clinics and notes from 2001–2005)

Grunsven, van Anky (adviser and demonstration rider)

Horse Event (numerous readings and clinics that have inspired us)

Has Den Bosch (partner, Talenten Kijkwizjzer)

Jansen-Bouwmeester, Inge (adviser, chapter 4)

Janssen, Sjef (adviser and participant in debates and discussions)

Jetten, Gertrud (adviser and editor)

KNHS (projects and discussions)

Kyrklund, Kyra (inspiration for chapters 3, 4, and 6)

McLean, Andrew and Manuele (advisers, chapter 5)

Murphy, Peter (adviser, chapter 3)

NHB Deurne (partner)

Noc-Nsf (adviser and Master Coach training)

Schuijer, Rico (adviser, chapter 3)

Sloet van Oldruitenborgh, Marianne (adviser, charts)

Stichting Hippische Innovatieve Projecten, and its sponsors and donors (advisers)

Veterinary Faculty at the University of Utrecht (data and training method examinations)

Voest, Emiel (adviser, chapter 2)

Weis, Richard (adviser, chapter 3)

Withages, Mariette (for inspiring and initiating the use of the term "Happy Athlete")

# Index